George W. Bush

George W. Bush

FROM TEXAS TO THE WHITE HOUSE

LIBBY HUGHES

FRANKLIN WATTS
A Division of Scholastic Inc.
New York Toronto London Auckland Sydney
Mexico City New Delhi Hong Kong
Danbury, Connecticut

To Mary Ellen, Amanda, Rebecca, and Abbie

ACKNOWLEDGEMENTS

My agent, Alison Picard; my editor, Wendy Mead; Betsey Welton; Stacey Silva; Peter and Caroline Vanderhoef; Georgia Dearborn; Kate Dearborn; Betsy Haney; Pat Adams; Marilyn Harrison; Mrs. Jenna Welch; Pat Owsley; April Burney; Bill Carlile; Nancy McKinley; Betty Orbeck; Charlene Gnagy; Todd Houck and Lisa Harrington from Midland's Petroleum Museum; Dr. Charles Younger; Lou Perkins; Tana Sherman; Reverend Charles Lutrick; and George P. Shultz, former secretary of state under President Ronald Reagan and Vice President George H.W. Bush.

Photographs © 2003: AP/Wide World Photos: 2 (Ron Heflin), 103 (Doug Mills), 59 (David J. Phillip); Corbis Images: back cover, 69, 85, 98, 107 (AFP), 32, 52 (Bettman), cover, 96, 110 (Reuters NewMedia Inc.), 74 (Joseph Sohm; ChromoSohm Inc.), 9; Corbis Sygma: 81, 86 (Bob Daemmrich), 94 (Kennerly David Hume); George Bush Presidential Library: 6, 14, 16, 17, 19, 40, 62, 64, 67, 78; Getty Images: 109 (Larry Downing/Reuters), 71 (Cynthia Johnson/Liaison), 93 (Adrees A. Latif/Reuters), 34 bottom (Darren McCollester/Newsmakers), 50 (Texas Air National Guard/Newsmakers), 100 (Rick Wilking/Liaison); Libby Hughes: 10, 12, 24; Manuscripts and Archives, Yale University Library: 45; Phillips Academy: 28, 34 top; The State Preservation Board, Austin, Texas: 84; Yale University/Michael Marsland: 36.

Library of Congress Cataloging-in-Publication Data
Hughes, Libby
George W. Bush: from Texas to the White House / by Libby Hughes
   p. cm. — (Great life stories)
Includes bibliographical references and index.
ISBN 0-531-12310-3
1. Bush, George W. (George Walker), 1946—Juvenile literature. 2. Presidents—United States—Biography—Juvenile literature. 3. Governors—Texas—Biography—Juvenile literature. 4. Children of presidents—United States—Biography—Juvenile literature. I. Title. II. Series.
E903 .H84 2003
973.931/092 B 21
                                                                                                    2003000957

Contents

Mr. and Mrs. George H.W. Bush gaze proudly at their firstborn son, George Walker Bush, on the campus of Yale University in New Haven, Connecticut, in April 1947. The elder Bush began his college career at Yale after he returned from World War II.

ONE

Born to Love Baseball

The most powerful influence on George W. Bush's life would be his parents and grandparents. He was born into a family of wealth and privilege. He was expected to live up to the highest qualities of character, integrity, and loyalty. There would be some bumpy places on the road from boyhood to manhood, but he would fulfill these family expectations. In politics, he would also follow closely in the footsteps of his grandfather, Prescott Bush—a United States senator from Connecticut—and his father, George Herbert Walker Bush—the forty-first president of the United States.

Before World War II ended, the elder George Bush came back from the South Pacific a hero as a fighter pilot. He quickly married his teenage sweetheart, Barbara Pierce, and headed to Yale University to study economics. There he became an outstanding student and a star athlete. However, for Barbara and George Bush, nothing could compare to the birth of their firstborn son, George Walker Bush, on July 6, 1946, at a hospital in New Haven, Connecticut. Soon the proud parents were taking their baby boy to Yale baseball and football games, introducing him to the love of sports almost from birth.

TEXAS, HERE WE COME!

After the elder George Bush graduated with his Phi Beta Kappa key (an award for outstanding scholarship), he had to find a job to support his family. Working as an investment broker on Wall Street, like his father had, did not interest him. George H. W. Bush wanted something more exciting. A family friend, Neil Mallon (also a Yale man), found him a job

Yale: A Family Tradition

Yale University dates back to 1701. It was formed by a group of ministers who felt that Harvard University had become too liberal. Set in the heart of New Haven, the gray-washed buildings were patterned after the Gothic architecture of Oxford and Cambridge Universities in England. The Yale atmosphere reflected a sense of stability and dedication to higher learning.

It was a tradition in the Bush family to attend Yale University. George W.'s grandfather Prescott Bush, and his uncle Prescott Bush, Jr., and his father were Yale graduates. Later, George W. and his daughter Barbara would continue the tradition.

at International Derrick & Equipment Company (IDECO) located in Odessa, Texas. Driving out to West Texas in his new maroon Studebaker car (a graduation present from his parents), George Bush arrived in the sweltering heat of summer. He found a small two-room apartment, where they shared a bathroom with another couple. Then he sent for Barbara and two-year-old George. After two more moves, the family settled into a small, gray ranch-style house at 916 East 17th Street, not far from the town's main street, Grant Avenue.

Texas is big. It is so large that it often seems like an entire country onto itself. Shaped a bit like a sheriff's badge, the Lone Star state has a variety of landscapes from the lush, hilly country in central Texas to the flat, dry plains of West Texas. The Spaniards had first explored Texas in 1519 and established settlements in 1635. The state has a long and colorful history, often pictured in movies. One could imagine the thunder of

A World War II hero returns to marry his sweetheart. Navy Lt. George H.W. Bush walks his bride, Barbara Pierce Bush, down the aisle of the First Presbyterian Church in Rye, New York.

Texas Oil

In the 1880s, a British geologist compared the rich formations of the land in West Texas with the Russian province of Perm. He found the two regions nearly identical. This part of West Texas became known as the Permian Basin, a place rich with oil and gas deposits. The town that grew up in the area was named *Odessa* after Odessa, Russia.

More than 250 million years ago, the Permian Basin was a shallow sea. By the twentieth century the sea had long since dried up. Rich pools of oil and gas were found in 1926, creating an oil boom. Many speculators from the east and west came to drill for this "black gold."

The young Bush family settled into a small ranch-style house at 916 East 17th Street in Odessa, Texas, in 1948.

cattle and galloping horses, ridden by cowboys silhouetted against a scarlet sky.

Far different from the greenery of New England, Odessa, Texas, was a desolate, flat plain under a dome of blue sky. The dust storms in March and April were legendary. They started on the distant horizon, brown dust moving on the hot wind across the plain in a blinding cloud. It rained mud. Everyone tried to rush indoors to safety. Then, after two hours, it was over, but the taste and smell of dirt would hang in the air for days. Dust would be left everywhere inside cars, homes, clothes, and hair. Barbara Bush found the hot winds and blowing sands a challenge. Even the smell of oil and gas was strange, but she was as much a pioneer as her husband.

The first year in Texas, George Bush swept floors and painted oil machinery in the 103 degree Fahrenheit (39.4 degree Celsius) temperatures. The work was hard, but he was learning about the oil business. The Bushes began to make friends and found themselves liking the wild, harsh surroundings. But soon there would be changes.

TO CALIFORNIA AND BACK TO TEXAS

By 1949, George Bush was transferred to California to sell oil-drilling equipment. There, the Bushes added a new baby girl to their family, Pauline Robinson Bush, nicknamed Robin. George adored his little sister.

The Bushes returned to West Texas in 1950. Instead of Odessa, they settled in Midland, Texas, a larger and more sophisticated place than Odessa. There, a small cluster of modest skyscrapers rise into the West Texas sky. In Midland, the oil companies had their administrative offices. There were golf courses, schools, parks, and movie theaters to entertain residents.

Midland was definitely an oil city, or "Tall City" as it was nick-named. Across the dry landscape, there were three thousand oil-drilling machines. The pumping units looked like giant insects, plunging their stingers deep into the earth.

The Bushes found a small, blue house on a dirt road at 405 East Maple Street. This street was called Easter Egg Row because all the

From 1950 to 1951, the Bushes lived at 405 East Maple Street in Midland, Texas. The cluster of houses was called Easter Egg Row because all the houses were painted in bright colors.

houses were painted bright colors. The Bushes wanted little George to have a backyard to play in, even though there weren't any trees.

At first, George Bush worked as a salesman for Dresser Industries in Midland. Then he decided to start his own business with his neighbor John Overbey. Bush's uncle, Herbert Walker, provided $300,000 of his own money and received additional funds from London investors to help start the company. Prescott Bush also put in $50,000. By 1953 they added two more partners and called the company "Zapata" after *Viva Zapata!*—a Marlon Brando movie about a Mexican revolutionary, who championed the cause of "land and liberty." In 1953 the Bush family also grew with the arrival of John Ellis Bush called "Jeb." With a growing family, the Bushes moved to 1412 West Ohio Street, nearer Midland's downtown area. In the same year, however, tragedy would strike the Bush family.

THE LOSS OF A SISTER

Robin was diagnosed with leukemia, a serious blood disease. George and Barbara took her to a hospital in New York City. A nanny was hired to look after George and Jeb because Barbara wanted to stay by Robin's bedside. The elder George commuted from Texas to New York every weekend. When Robin died at the age of four, her parents were shocked and heartbroken. They decided not to tell young George until they could see him face to face.

His parents flew back to Midland and drove to the Sam Houston Elementary School. Seven-year-old George saw the car and asked his teacher if he could go out to see his parents and little sister. He rushed

Father and son pose together outside their 1412 W. Ohio St. home in Midland, Texas, in 1954.

out to the car to greet his parents, but Robin wasn't there. His parents told him that she would never be there. She had died from leukemia. Young George and his parents wept.

George couldn't believe that he would never see Robin again. He was crushed. He had always had a protective feeling about Robin and was proud to be her brother. Over the weeks and months, young George could sense his mother's grief over the loss of her daughter. To help his mother overcome her sorrow, he would try to be funny, hoping to make her laugh and take her mind off the loss. One Saturday, a friend came over, wanting George to play. At the screen door, he told the friend, "I can't come out and play. I have to play with my mother. She's lonely."

The elder George Bush missed his daughter too. But he and Barbara had to deal with their emotional pain. After all, they had two little boys to raise. Despite their sorrow, the family moved ahead with their lives.

A Texas Boyhood

Midland, Texas, was an ideal place for a young boy. It was family oriented and safe. From the three-bedroom house at 1412 West Ohio Street, George could hop on his bicycle and ride with his friends or go over to the Ritz movie theater. He could walk to the one-story yellow brick Sam Houston Elementary School, which was located behind the Memorial Stadium and beside the large Baptist Church. His favorite sport was Little League baseball, and baseball star Willy Mays was his hero. Barbara willingly drove George to all the games and his father came, too, when he wasn't away on business. Because of her husband's many absences, much of the discipline was left to Barbara. After Robin's death, Barbara was very protective of young George.

Nevertheless, young George was full of mischief and had a certain wild streak. He brought excitement to his younger brothers, who couldn't

George W. Bush, pictured in 1954, had dreams of becoming a baseball player during his Little League days in Midland, Texas. His hero was Willy Mays.

wait until he came home from school. When the screen door slammed, they knew who it was. His brothers jumped up and down, wanting to know what games George had planned for them. He was also a prankster and loved playing tricks on his brothers and his friends.

TEXAS, A FRIENDLY STATE

For the Bushes life in Texas was very different than New England. Winters were mild. Deals were made in the coffee shop of the six-story Scharbauer Hotel or at Agnes' Cafe. For Midland families, there were many backyard barbecues with friends. Good food, interesting stories, and laughter were all part of Texas culture.

In Midland, church was at the center of the Bushes' lives, as it was for many southerners. Aside from services, there were church socials and big church suppers. The whole family went to church, and no one had to be pushed. The Bushes attended the First Presbyterian Church in Odessa and in Midland. Big George taught Sunday school. On Wednesday evenings, he and Barbara attended prayer meetings.

The Bush parents were active in the community as a whole. They participated in

Now a family of six, the Bushes pose for a photograph in Houston, Texas, in 1959.

local theater productions, worked at the YMCA or local hospitals, and helped raise funds for charities. George Bush was also an ardent Republican, trying to rally support in a Democratic state.

All in all, it was a happy life, and the family continued to grow. Soon, two more brothers would join George and Jeb. In 1954 Neil Mallon Bush was born, followed by Marvin Pierce Bush in 1956.

As the family grew and the business prospered, they built a long, low ranch-style house at 2703 Sentinel. Behind the house was an old buffalo wallow that had been turned into a park with a baseball field. George W. was there every day after school until the last fading light of day. Often his father played with the neighborhood boys, delighting them by catching a ball in a mitt behind his back. They tried hard to copy him, but without much success.

Summers in Texas could be brutally hot. Some Texans retreated to cooler places such as Colorado, Wyoming, or Maine while others just weathered the heat. The Bushes usually sent George and the boys to Camp Longhorn in the hill country of central Texas in July. One of the campers, whom young George did not know at the time, was a girl by the name of Kay Bailey. Later in life, she would become Republican Senator Kay Bailey Hutchison from Texas and a good friend to George W. Bush.

ESCAPE TO MAINE

Almost every August, Barbara would drive the boys from Midland to Kennebunkport, Maine, for a few weeks. Maine was cool and comfortable in summer. A breeze always came off the ocean. Along the rocky coastline, there was a strong smell of salt, fish, and seaweed. Hotels and huge houses lined the beachfront. Kennebunkport, a small town on the southern coast of Maine, had a winding main street of quaint shops, seafood restaurants, and ice cream parlors for rainy days. As a teenager, George W. would rush out to the local fish market to order lobsters.

George's grandparents, Prescott and Dorothy Walker Bush, had a large family compound on Ocean Avenue. It sat out on a rocky peninsula, with a stone jetty that pointed its long finger into the Atlantic Ocean. During stormy weather, the waves crashed against the rocks,

Visiting George, little George, and Barbara in West Texas, in 1950, were George W.'s grandparents, Prescott Bush and Dorothy Walker Bush.

shooting sea spray high into the air. Named Walker's Point for Dorothy Walker Bush's family, the big house had many bedrooms and a huge fireplace for cool summer evenings.

George's grandmother was a competitive sportswoman. She played a fierce game of tennis and would swim in the cold waters of the Atlantic Ocean. She organized lots of activities for the grandchildren when they came to visit, including swimming, fishing, and outdoor games. At night or on rainy days, there was backgammon, chess, or tiddly winks. Since grandfather Bush was very tall and a disciplinarian, he insisted the children speak politely and dress formally for dinner. Young George, who always wore informal dress in Texas, was a little frightened by his six-foot-four grandfather.

In her autobiography, Barbara Bush described the long drive from Texas to Maine. Sometimes she would take one or two African American maids to help her with the children. Because the United States was still racially segregated during those years, Barbara's black maids were not allowed to be served in white restaurants. Restrooms and drinking fountains were labeled with signs for "whites" and for "coloreds." Instead of making the maids sit in the car and wait, Barbara bought food so that they could all picnic together.

When young George was growing up in Midland, the races were segregated. He had little opportunity to meet and mix with African Americans and Hispanics. Later, in his autobiography, George W. Bush recalled unfavorable racial comments made by friends in his elementary school. When he repeated these remarks in front of his mother, she washed his mouth out with soap, lectured him about racial prejudice, and instructed him never to say such things again. The Bushes would not tolerate that kind of behavior toward any minority. Both Barbara and George Bush had been raised by parents who had taught them racial tolerance. During the 1940s and 1950s, even though many people were still racially prejudiced, the Bushes insisted that their children show respect to African Americans and Hispanics.

Riding bikes around Midland with friends, playing baseball, and going to movies was about to end for young George and his family. George Bush's business was booming. He was buying new, tripod oil rigs for offshore drilling, but Midland was a long way from the water. The Bush family decided to move to Houston, located in the southeast part of Texas, near the Gulf of Mexico.

LIFE IN HOUSTON

Compared to Midland, Houston was huge. The city was named for General Sam Houston, a Texas hero who defeated the Mexican Army on a nearby battlefield in 1845. From a cotton and cattle center, Houston

Separate, but Not Equal

Segregation was a policy of keeping races separate. The United States began taking steps to end the policy of segregation in the 1950s. In 1954, the Supreme Court ruled that segregation in schools was unconstitutional. By 1957, President Dwight D. Eisenhower ordered the U.S. Army to escort black children safely into the schools of Little Rock, Arkansas. The city of Houston, Texas, began integrating its elementary schools in 1960.

had become a hub for oil, steel, and chemicals. Skyscrapers rose like giant fingers from the flat coastal plains. This was not the place for cowboys. It was a city for businessmen.

The Lyndon B. Johnson Space Center (NASA) is located in Houston. Rice University, the University of Houston, Texas Southern University are only a few of the twenty-five educational institutions located there. The city is also home to many museums and performing arts groups as well as a world-renowned medical center.

In 1959 George and Barbara bought an acre of wooded land at 5525 Brian Drive in Houston where they would build a house for their large family. The boys would have a swimming pool, a baseball diamond, and rubber tire swings to provide outlets for their energy. They couldn't afford to be in the wealthy Tanglewood area, but this was a very good neighborhood.

The Bushes discovered that they already knew one of their neighbors. Peter Vanderhoef, George H. W. Bush's childhood friend from Greenwich Country Day School in Connecticut, lived right behind them. Barbara Bush had even once gone on a date once with Peter to a country club on Hope Sound in Rye, New York.

Soon after the move to Houston in August of 1959, the four Bush brothers would have a new sister, Dorothy Walker Bush, nicknamed Doro. The family would always miss Robin, but they were glad to have a new daughter and sister to cherish.

George never forgot his old friends, but he had a great capacity for making new ones. His parents decided to enroll him in the Kinkaid private school in Houston. He had finished seventh grade in Midland and entered Kinkaid for eighth and ninth grades. Although not as socially or academically prestigious as St. John's School in Houston, Kinkaid was a good private school. George fit in perfectly at Kinkaid.

HOUSTON'S SOCIAL LIFE

The Bushes felt comfortable in Houston. In many ways, Houston society in the 1940s, 1950s, and 1960s was much like Greenwich, Connecticut. The cities were quite different, but both societies were rich, sophisticated, and cultured. Men wore suits and ties and women wore elegant dresses to social events. While Greenwich had families that had been rich for generations after generations, many of Houston's rich became wealthy quickly from oil. The population of Houston was larger and more diverse than Greenwich— it had a larger cross section of people from different classes and races.

Both places offered a country club life for some of the residents. The Bushes belonged to the prestigious Houston Country Club. Each year, the club would be the site for many debutante parties. Debutantes, carefully selected by the Allegro Club, were young women presented to Houston society in the ballroom of the club. However, the Bushes were not as interested as many members were in fancy parties. Mostly, club membership gave the family a place to eat, a place for their children to swim, and a place to meet friends.

Businessmen met downtown at the exclusive Houston Club or at the Petroleum Club for lunch or dinner. Here, they would make business deals under more elegant conditions than those in Midland. Many wealthy oil executives helped support opera, ballet, and theater.

Although fifteen-year-old George W. Bush liked Houston, he would not stay there very long.

This photograph shows the chapel at Phillips Academy, a distinguished boys' private school, in Andover, Massachusetts, where George W. attended from 1961 to 1964.

THREE

Eastern Weather and Ways

Members of the Bush family were expected to follow tradition. George H. W. Bush, his brother, and many cousins had attended one of the oldest private boarding schools for young men in the United States, Phillips Academy in Andover, Massachusetts. There, he distinguished himself as an outstanding sportsman and student. His parents and professors expected him to go from Andover to Yale, which he did after World War II.

There was no question that George W. Bush would go to Andover too. Of course, George's Texas friends thought he was sent there because he was a wild sort of kid. For many years, southern families had sent their poorly behaved children to schools up north to straighten them out. That wasn't the case with George. He was just expected to follow in his father's footsteps.

Phillips Academy, located 25 miles (40.2 kilometers) northwest of Boston, was founded in 1778. George Washington delivered an address there, and his nephews attended the school. Among 500 acres (202.3 hectares) of rolling land, the school's redbrick buildings—examples of early American architecture—are surrounded by maple and elm trees, pink cherry trees, and white dogwood. In the middle of the Front Lawn, the bell tower dominates both the campus and the quaint town.

The new sophomore who arrived in 1961 from Texas was assigned to Bancroft dormitory. John Kidde, a football and soccer player from Pasadena, California, was his roommate. At first, George was homesick for his family, so he gravitated to the eighteen Texans who also went to school at Andover to lessen the pain of missing those he loved. But he soon overcame those feelings.

A New Young President

While George W. Bush was settling in at Phillips Academy in 1961, a relatively young man from Massachusetts, John F. Kennedy, was beginning his first term as the thirty-fifth president of the United States. One of his goals was to put the first human on the moon through the U.S. space program. Although the Soviet Union's Yuri Gagarin was the first man in space in 1961, the United States launched Navy Commander Alan B. Shepard, Jr. into space for fifteen minutes a few weeks later.

LIFE AT ANDOVER

Meanwhile, the transition from the hot, humid weather of Houston to the cold, damp winters of Massachusetts was a shock to George. Andover gave George a real taste of winter's cutting winds and drifting snow. He had to change the way he dressed too—and not just because of the weather. The relaxed informality of blue jeans and cowboy boots worn in Texas contrasted sharply with the coat, shirt, and tie required for class attendance at Phillips.

In spite of the cold weather and formal dress code, George did what he had always done best—made friends. His Kinkaid friends had marveled at the way George could work a room full of people when he was thirteen and fourteen years old. He moved skillfully through a big crowd, speaking a few words to everyone. He used the same method at Andover. Everywhere on campus, George set his winning Texas ways in motion. He introduced himself to each new person he met. Since there were fewer than one thousand students, he had met most of them by the end of his first semester.

The students at Phillips Academy were surprised by this southerner, who grabbed their elbows, shook their hands, and introduced himself. They were both startled and charmed by the newcomer. A hockey player from Michigan, Bill Semple, has recalled George W. during their Andover days. "George was always part of a small group of seven or eight guys who were really . . . the big men on campus. He just didn't let people get to know him. . . . He managed to get himself in the right place at the right time."

George W. Bush was the head cheerleader at Phillips Academy. He and his eight other male cheerleaders stuffed themselves into and around a telephone booth.

Andover boys responded to George's whirlwind of fun. A certain excitement followed him wherever he went on campus. Fellow students liked to be around him. He teased, he laughed, and he joked. Life was one long party around George. But there were serious times too.

Essentially, Phillips was a place to study and learn. There were no distractions of coed classes. Female students weren't admitted until 1973 when the all-girls' school, Abbot Academy, in Andover merged with Phillips. George W. admits that he was not the greatest student. His best grades came from the subjects that interested him. They were history, math, and Spanish. He credits his history teacher, Ted Lyons, for sparking his interest in history. Lyons, a one-time football player, had contracted polio, a disabling disease, at Brown University. Yet he never let his disability prevent him from imparting his love of history to his students in his classroom at Samuel Phillips Hall. He was an inspiration to George.

Sometimes, to finish his homework, George would stretch out on the floor after lights out at 10:00 P.M. to read or write by the light coming under his door from the hallway.

HUMILIATION IN CLASS

During his first year at Andover, George had to work hard to keep up with his assignments. He set out to impress his English teacher with a paper describing the death of his sister Robin. He used a thesaurus to find bigger words to use. But when the paper came back, a great big zero was marked on it and the word *disgraceful* written in bold letters. George had chosen the word *lacerates* instead of *tears* to express his feelings about Robin. That was a humiliating experience, but he learned a huge lesson about writing simply and not trying to impress instructors.

Besides studying and doing his homework, George pursued his interest in athletics. From boyhood, George had always loved competitive sports. He and fellow Texan, Clay Johnson, were on the second string

Beatlemania

In 1962, a sensational singing group called The Beatles was starting to make it big. The four boys from Liverpool, England, wearing bushy, Dutch boy haircuts, captured the imagination of British and American young people. They were as popular, if not more so, than Elvis Presley was. Even George W. Bush once did his own impersonation of them by wearing a mop on his head at a stickball rally on the Andover campus.

of Andover's junior varsity basketball and baseball teams, but rarely did they move off the bench. The younger Bush didn't qualify as a first-rate athlete like his father.

A SUMMER JOB

At the end of his sophomore year, his parents arranged for George to work on a friend's dude ranch in Arizona. There he built corral fences to keep the cattle contained. George earned $200 a month. It was apparent to his roommate Peter Neumann, a nephew of the ranch owner, that George worshipped his father and thought everything he did was perfection. George wanted to be just like his father. The sixteen-year-old son confided that he thought his father would be president one day.

This attitude toward his father was unusual. Most teenagers have strained relationships with their parents during this stage of life and many behave in a rebellious manner—but not George. His loyalty to his family was very deep, and that would never change. George always admired his father.

When George W. returned for his junior year at Andover, he stayed in America House, down the hill from the main campus. This was a wood-frame dormitory with black shutters. Samuel F. Smith, who penned the words to the song "America" in 1832, had lived and composed lyrics in this house over a century before. In his senior year, George was made a proctor—someone responsible for seeing that the rules of the dormitory are enforced.

Headmaster John Kemper, a graduate of the U.S. Military Academy at West Point, wanted students at Andover to strive for excellence in academics and to have "a sense of humanity and public service." However, many of the young men thought it was smart to be sarcastic about teachers or other students. (Kemper may not have approved of this kind of humor.) Perhaps this is how George W. developed his lifelong habit of giving people nicknames. Sometimes the names were not flattering, but they were given with humor, not malice, and they delighted his friends. Some of the names were Squirt, Bear, Mr. Babar, Spider, Moondoggie, Crusader, and Critter.

Although there were only a few African American students at Andover, racial prejudice was not tolerated, as it was not tolerated in the Bush household. George had learned that every individual mattered whatever the color of his skin. His father had told him that everyone in our country should have equal opportunity to apply for any job. There were demonstrations in the United States during the 1960s for greater

Martin Luther King, Jr.'s "I Have a Dream" Speech

In the late summer of 1963, 200,000 people filled the mall around the Washington Monument in Washington, D.C., to demand passage of civil rights legislation. From the columns of the Lincoln Memorial, Dr. Martin Luther King, Jr.'s words echoed through the loudspeaker system. "I still have a dream that one day this nation will rise up and live out the true meaning of its creed: 'We hold these truths to be self-evident, that all men are created equal.'"

equality. Sometimes the demonstrations were non-violent, and sometimes they weren't. The news of the day was filled with the struggle for civil rights.

In November of 1963, the nation mourned when President John F. Kennedy was assassinated in Dallas, Texas. Kennedy had only three short years as president. George and his friends were stunned by the news. They put aside their cheerful pranks to think deeply about such a terrible act. Party ideology did not enter into the feeling of grief that George felt over the nation's loss and the loss to Kennedy's family, wife, and children. He especially regretted that the incident took place in Texas.

Kennedy's vice president, Lyndon Baines Johnson, a Texan, was sworn in as president on the same day Kennedy died in 1963. When George was six years old, he had met Johnson. George was visiting his grandfather, Senator Prescott Bush, in Washington, D.C. Senator Bush

President and Mrs. John Kennedy ride in a motorcade in Dallas, Texas, on November 22, 1963. This photo was taken only minutes before the president was assassinated.

introduced his grandson to Senator Johnson from Texas. To a little boy, everything about Johnson seemed larger than life. He was taller than average. He had big hands and a booming voice. George never forgot that moment. Later in life, he admired Johnson for his war against poverty and his concern for the disadvantaged.

A FOOTBALL CHEERLEADER

At all school games, George headed an eight-person cheerleading group to support the football and baseball teams. What George lacked as an athlete, he made up for by revving up the mood of the crowds at games. This cheerleading may have been good training for his future in politics.

After the winter doldrums of his senior year, George had an idea. He stood up at an assembly meeting in the chapel to suggest forming a stickball league among the various dormitory halls. The response was enthusiastic. George declared himself the "high commissioner." Using balls and broomstick handles, the players on each team were very competitive. As the stickball high commissioner, Bush nicknamed himself "Tweeds Bush" for William "Boss" Tweed, a notorious political boss of New York City in the 1800s.

When colleges were making their decisions about accepting incoming freshmen, Andover boys were full of anxiety. George spoke with the dean of students about going to Yale. He wasn't sure if Yale would accept his "C" average. The dean suggested that, as a back-up, he submit his application to another college. To prepare for Yale's rejection, George began talking about possibly going to the University of Texas. Despite his fears and his worry about disappointing his father, an

The Andover cheerleader, George W. Bush, belts out encouraging cheers from his megaphone for the Phillips Academy football team. At Ground Zero in New York on September 11, 2001, he would use another microphone to cheer the firefighters and police officers, digging through the remains of the World Trade Center in New York.

GEORGE WALKER BUSH
"Tweeds" "Lip"
5525 BRIAN DRIVE, HOUSTON, TEXAS

YALE   LOWER
JULY 6, 1946   AMERICA

JV Baseball 2,3; Varsity Baseball 4; JV Basketball 2,3; Varsity Basket-ball 4; JV Football 3,4; Head Cheerleader 4; Athletic Advisory Board 4; Student Congress 4; Spanish Club 2,3,4; Phillips Society 2,3,4; Stick-ball Commission 3,4; High Commissioner of Stickball 4; Proctor, Amer-ica House.

Roommate: John Kidde

The 1964 yearbook photograph shows a young George W. Bush soon to graduate from Phillips Academy.

envelope arrived from Yale, containing George's acceptance letter.

During the graduation ceremonies at Phillips Academy, the graduates listened to John Kemper deliver remarks on the steps in front of Samuel Phillips Hall. Afterwards, the young men formed a circle on the grounds below, while their parents stood behind them. Each time a graduate received his diploma, he stepped back from the circle.

After George graduated from Phillips in 1964, he returned to Texas for the summer to work in his father's campaign for senator from Texas against Democrat Ralph Yarborough. It was a busy summer. He delivered signs to different towns. He made up a list of key people running his father's campaign in each town and listed facts about each county. There were telephone numbers to gather and other small jobs that no one else would do, but they were important. George's job as a cheerleader at Andover helped prepare him for organizing political rallies for his father. During the summer, they traveled to forty cities in Texas.

When summer was over, it was time for George to start his freshman year at Yale.

Not until his sophomore year at Yale University, in 1965, would George W. Bush live at Davenport College, a student residence, where he would live for three more years.

FOUR

Living It Up at Yale

Again, George W. Bush was to follow family tradition. He would become the third generation of Bush men to attend Yale University and cheer for the Yale football team. Prescott Bush and George Herbert Walker had blazed the Yale pathway for George H. W. Bush and his son. George W. had completed Phillips Academy as his father had. He was neither an academic nor an athletic star, but he made a lasting impression on the students and faculty. And he had gained some lifelong friends.

In the fall of 1964, George headed north to the Gothic towers and cloistered buildings of Yale University in New Haven, Connecticut. New Haven is a town that sits on the Atlantic Ocean, surrounded by suburbs, not far from New York City. Yale has a life of its own, apart from the city and the world.

George W.'s arrival on the Yale campus was quite different from that of his father. His father had been a married man and had spent several years fighting a war in the South Pacific. He had come to Yale as a more mature man with a family to support. His son came to the university as a boy with only limited real-life experiences.

As a student, George W. may not have brought the brilliance of his father and two grandfathers to the aristocratic institution. But he brought the same social qualities to Yale that he used at Phillips Academy. Within months, many Yalies knew who George W. Bush was because he shook a new hand wherever he found one.

Bush and two of his friends from Phillips Academy became roommates on the Old Campus at Yale. Andover graduate Clay Johnson from Fort Worth, Texas, and Robert Dieter from Florida shared a suite with George.

LIBERAL POLITICS AT YALE

While George had been campaigning for his father in Texas, the country was absorbed by the national election for president. Arizona Republican Barry Goldwater was running against Texas Democrat Lyndon B. Johnson. When Yale students were polled for their preference, the results showed almost 75 percent for Johnson. Also, in a mock poll for the Texas senate race, Yarborough won over the elder Bush. It was a bitter result for the younger Bush. However, George W. remained loyal to the conservative philosophy and felt the Yalies were too liberal and intellectually arrogant.

Interrupting the start of his freshman year at Yale, George W. flew back to Texas in November to help tally the election-night results in the banquet room of the Hotel America in Houston. His father's election to the senate was his first priority. But the criticism that had been leveled at his father throughout the campaign by the Houston Democrats angered and hurt George W. They had called his father a rich easterner and a carpetbagger—an unflattering term from the Civil War describing someone from the North who came to the South to sell his wares. Ralph Yarborough won the senate seat. Yarborough defeated Bush by 300,000 votes, or a 12 percent margin. Barbara Bush couldn't hold back the tears as she stood behind her husband, listening to his concession speech. George W. held his tears until they were in private. Then his disappointment and emotion overflowed. For a son who idolized his father, defeat was difficult to accept. Over the years, he grew to understand the role of defeat in the rough world of politics, but it was never easy for him to hear his own father criticized at any time.

After George flew back to Yale, he did not talk about his father's loss. However, one day on campus, he ran into William Sloane Coffin, Jr., Yale's chaplain and a well-known liberal. Coffin had been a classmate of his father, and they both were members of a secret society at Yale called Skull and Bones. George W. introduced himself to Coffin and told him that his father had just suffered a political defeat by Ralph Yarborough for a senate seat in Texas.

"He was beaten by a better man," said Coffin. George carried that stinging remark with him. When George referred to the incident thirty years later, Coffin wrote him a note to apologize and said that he didn't

Carefree and happy, George Bush wears his Yale baseball cap as he crosses the Yale campus.

even remember saying such a thing. George wrote back that he remembered every word, but he bore Coffin no ill will. This was an example of George's loyalty to his father and his inability to forget a personal attack against him.

Once George put Texas politics behind him, he resumed campus life at Yale. Strangely, he never joined the young Republican Club at Yale or ever debated politics with his fellow students. Instead, he concentrated on his social skills and his studies. Some observers have speculated that he was protecting his political ideas for a future time.

The structure and study habits he gained at Andover helped George at Yale. No one was there to supervise his study time. He had to do it all himself. His courses were a mix of political science, history, philosophy, Spanish, and a smattering of science courses. Although he loved sports, he wasn't good enough to make the first-string teams, but he always supported the teams and intramural sports. He did manage to make the first team in rugby by his senior year, but he just couldn't measure up to his father in baseball or in academics. Nevertheless, he worked hard and played hard, hurrying from class to class as the bells in Harkness Tower rang out twice a day.

DISAPPOINTING HIS FATHER

George's father had a plan for his son during the summer of 1965. He thought it would be a good idea for his son to work on an oil-drilling rig for Circle Drilling Company. Under the blazing sun in southern Louisiana, George worked a ten-day shift—ten days of hard work and ten days to go home to rest, play tennis, and party. Or he would work a seven-day shift with seven days off. It was hard physical labor.

As the summer was coming to an end, George decided to quit seven days before he returned to Yale. When his father heard the news, he demanded that his son come to his office in Houston. In quiet tones, the older Bush said, "You agreed to work a certain amount of time, and you didn't. I just wanted you to know that you have disappointed me."

George was devastated. Any sort of physical punishment would have been better. To have your own father, whom you loved and revered, tell you that he was disappointed in you was a far greater punishment. One that he would always remember. From that experience, he learned to honor and keep his commitments no matter what they were.

Back at Yale, sophomores were assigned to twelve residential colleges, similar to Great Britain's system at Oxford and Cambridge Universities. George and his buddies Clay Johnson, Rob Dieter, Terry

Johnson (no relation to Clay), and Ted Livingston found themselves at Davenport College. Davenport was not known for its intellectual geniuses. Its nickname was "Jock College." The residents were considered party boys and sports jocks.

The Bush roommates decided to try to join the Delta Kappa Epsilon (DKE) fraternity on nearby York Street. George's father had been a member during his Yale years. Once George and his roommates were accepted as pledges, they had to go through a hazing period. During this time, the pledges were humiliated and asked to do strange things. George's friends were told by DKE men to name all the pledges in the room. None of them could name more than four at the most. But George W. was able to name all fifty-four pledges. His grandfather, Prescott Bush, had the same gift for remembering names.

The Davenport suite occupied by George and his Andover buddies was the center of activity in the college. Wherever George was, things were happening. People wanted to be around this fun guy. They would talk about sports and girls. Or on the weekends, they would play poker all night. The suite was the gathering place for exchanging information because George knew what was going on all over campus. Through his social contacts across campus, he picked up the latest campus news. And through casual conversations with girls he knew which girls' schools were holding dances. George was also an organizer. He made arrangements for going to parties, dances, or sports events by car, bus, or train.

The summer of 1966 would bring George to a different job. This time he worked in the sports department at Sears in Houston for $212 a month. He loved it. He outsold everyone else until one of the regular employees asked him to stop. George was earning commissions that the other men could use to support their families. George understood and pulled back.

George had other interests too. He was becoming interested in a woman named Cathryn Wolfman, who had grown up in the Bush's neighborhood. She first attended Smith College in Massachusetts and then Rice University in Houston. She was bright and witty. Everyone considered her to be a great person to be around. George wanted to be around her a lot. They became engaged over Christmas of his junior year at Yale.

The Vietnam War

From 1955 to 1975, the United States tried to stop the communist North Vietnamese from taking over South Vietnam. The United States feared that all of Southeast Asia would fall to the communists. This was called the "Domino Theory." The United States supplied aid, advisers, and eventually troops and air power to South Vietnam to prevent communism from spreading across the border.

Many Americans were opposed to the war in Vietnam because the United States had not been directly attacked as it had been at Pearl Harbor in 1941. Many people felt the war was unwinnable because Americans didn't have the heart to win this kind of war. American universities were aflame with students protesting against the Vietnam War. While George was finishing his final year at Yale in 1967-1968, the Vietnam War was at its peak. U.S. troops were unable to gain a victory, and they started withdrawing in 1973. The North Vietnamese took over South Vietnam in 1975, making it part of their communist nation.

Also in 1966, the elder George Bush had decided to run for the congressional seat from Houston. This time, people listened to what he had to say, and he won the election. George was proud of his father for not giving up after his earlier defeat. The Bush family sold their big Houston house and bought a condominium to keep there. Then they moved to Washington, D.C.

THE YALE PRANKSTER

Meanwhile, George W. Bush was getting into trouble at Yale. When the school's football team, the Yale Bulldogs, met the Princeton team in New Jersey for the championship play-off, George W. was there to cheer as a loyal supporter. The Bulldogs won and the Yalies went crazy with excitement. Fans rushed the goal posts, and George straddled the crossbar, shouting and whooping his approval. However, the Princeton campus police were not pleased by this display of triumph. They ordered

Actor Becomes Governor

In 1966, Ronald Reagan, a former Hollywood actor, ran for governor in California. He won the election by a large margin and served two terms as governor. As governor, he spoke against higher taxes and encouraged welfare reform. Later Reagan would become the fortieth president of the United States with George H. W. Bush serving as his vice president.

George to the ground and herded the Yale boys off the field, demanding that they get out of town and stay out of town.

George, the fun-loving mischief maker, added another prank to his growing list. This time he and his friends were preparing for a Christmas party at the DKE house. While driving through town, George spotted a wreath on a New Haven hotel. He directed his buddies to go to the front entrance while he dismantled the wreath to use as a decoration for the fraternity house party. At that very moment, the police witnessed the theft of the wreath and apprehended them for disorderly conduct. After making an apology, George and his friends were released.

For George, the fraternity house was not only steps away from Davenport, but also the heart and center of his life. By his senior year, he became the DKE president. The DKEs were known for their parties. They hired big

This is Bush's yearbook photo at Yale when he graduated in 1968 as a history major.

bands and held creative costume parties. However, national debate about the worthiness of fraternities was discussed in the media at length. The practices of hazing and discrimination were widely denounced. The DKEs initiated its pledges by branding a Delta mark on their backs. There was an uproar in the press about it. In the face of the Vietnam War, fraternity life appeared rather frivolous. Nevertheless, the friendships George made among his fraternity brothers at Yale became lifelong relationships.

The Order of Skull and Bones

The Order of Skull and Bones is the oldest of seven secret societies at Yale. It was founded in 1832 by Yale student William Huntington Russell. Based on a society at a German university, Russell invited fourteen other young men in their junior year at Yale to join him as founding members. The "tomb" was built on High Street in 1856 as a dark and mysterious meeting place for the "Bonesmen" who still meet there every Thursday and Sunday in their senior year.

Skull and Bones members are expected to become leaders in their future careers, men of power in business, or government, and influential in all walks of life. Some of the famous names from the "Skull and Bones" society include Averill Harriman, businessman and politician; William F. Buckley, Jr., conservative Republican commentator and writer; Henry Luce, publisher of *Time* magazine; Senator John Kerry, Vietnam veteran and Democratic senator from Massachusetts; and a host of others. Since the 1950s a few Jews and African Americans have been invited to join, but no women.

While he was at Yale, George was uncertain whether he would be invited to join another organization, the secret society called the Order of the Skull and Bones. His father was a member, but George thought his less-than-impressive academic record might prevent him from getting an invitation. In case of rejection, he told his friends that he might join a different secret society.

The society only allows fifteen men from the junior class to join each year. They select new members on the last Thursday of April. When the April night arrived, George heard a knock on his door. It was someone—someone they thought might have been his father—to escort him to the tomb of the Skull and Bones. He became a member and, once again, followed in the family's traditions.

FIVE

A Pilot Goes to Harvard

Six months before graduating from Yale, George W. Bush gave serious thought to serving his country in the Vietnam War. Many students at Yale and other universities wanted to go to Canada to escape the draft into military service, but not Bush. Like his father, he would serve because he thought it was the right thing to do. Since his father loved flying, Bush decided at Christmas in 1967 to become a pilot. He learned that the Texas Air National Guard had openings. In January of 1968, he took his aptitude test at Westover Air Force Base in Massachusetts. By May, he had been accepted into the Texas Guard and started basic training at Lackland Air Force Base in San Antonio, Texas, during July and August. There wasn't time to enjoy his graduation from Yale.

A NATIONAL GUARD TRAINEE

After George completed his training, he was transferred to Valdosta, Georgia, to learn how to fly. He started with a small Cessna-type plane before moving up to the F-102 jet fighter. After fifty-five weeks in the Texas Air National Guard, Bush was awarded his wings as a second lieutenant. On December 29, 1969, his father proudly pinned the wings on his son. Now, they both shared the special joy of flying.

After graduating from Yale University, George W. Bush joined the Texas Air National Guard as a second lieutenant in 1968. His father proudly shows his son's officer bars at an official ceremony.

Meanwhile, Bush and his fiancée, Cathy Wolfman, couldn't seem to find a date for their wedding. They were leading separate lives and soon drifted apart. In spite of their parting, George always respected her.

WHAT TO DO NEXT?

During the early 1970s Bush was living in Houston and was assigned to Ellington Air Force Base. He eventually moved into a complex of apartments called Chateaux Dijon where many single young people lived. The trendy two-story stucco and white wood apartments were near the busy skyscrapers of Houston. One side was the quiet side, and the other was for the loud, party groups who played tennis, went swimming, or played water volleyball. Not until many years later would Bush discover

1968: A Tragic Year

The United States lost two prominent figures in 1968. On April 4, 1968, Dr. Martin Luther King, Jr., a leader of the Civil Rights Movement, was shot and killed in Memphis, Tennessee. King had won the 1964 Nobel Peace Prize for his work for racial equality.

A few months later, Robert Kennedy—a U.S. senator and presidential hopeful—was assassinated in Los Angeles, California. As a senator, Kennedy was a supporter of antipoverty programs, Medicare, and education. His death was yet another tragedy to strike the Kennedy family. His brother, President John F. Kennedy, had been assassinated only a few years earlier.

that a woman named Laura Welch lived on the quiet side. George was on the rowdy side. Their paths never crossed.

In 1970, Bush's father decided to make another run for the senate. This time he would be running against a well-known and well-respected Democrat, Lloyd Bentsen. The elder Bush lost again. The disappointment, however, was offset when President Richard M. Nixon appointed George H. W. Bush to be the ambassador to the United Nations. The Bushes were thrilled and moved to the Waldorf Astoria in New York City.

At this point in his life, Bush was floundering. He didn't know what to do next, except party long and hard. He applied to law schools in

Dorothy   Jeb   George Jr.   George   Barbara   Marvin   Neil

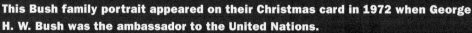

This Bush family portrait appeared on their Christmas card in 1972 when George H. W. Bush was the ambassador to the United Nations.

Austin and Houston, but was turned down by both. He worked for a family friend for a short time in the agriculture business, but that was not exciting enough for Bush.

By May of 1972, he had transferred his weekend duties with the National Guard to Montgomery, Alabama. There he became political director for Red Blount's campaign for the senate as a Republican. In those days, the American South was heavily Democratic. Republicans were considered Yankee outsiders. Blount lost to Democrat John Sparkman.

After the Alabama campaign, things began to come into focus for the younger Bush. He started working in Houston's inner city to help young African American kids. An African American friend, John White, asked Bush to be his assistant on Project PULL. Bush began to see some of life's hardships firsthand. Drugs, alcohol, teenage pregnancies, weapons, and abuse were daily occurrences in the Third Ward area of Houston. Bush befriended Jimmy, a five-year-old black boy, who was like his shadow. Years later the boy was murdered. This experience helped Bush form his future political philosophy that "no child should be left behind."

HARVARD BUSINESS SCHOOL

In the fall of 1973, Bush finished his National Guard service and arrived at the Harvard Business School in Cambridge, Massachusetts, to study business over the next two years. This time, he rented a small apartment in the area of Central Square. The business school was across the Charles River. Bush did not attend as many parties as in his earlier days. For pleasure, he went jogging and rode his bike. Aside from those small diversions, he studied conscientiously because his life seemed to have more purpose. The freewheeling social days of Andover and Yale were behind him. Bush and eighty others in his section at Harvard Business School learned how big businesses were organized and operated. They analyzed two or three case histories a night, studying until midnight or later. The Harvard Business School was fairly relaxed about a dress code. Some of the graduate students wore suits and ties, but Bush wore his flight bomber's jacket from the Texas Air National Guard over his shirt and tie.

George had many relatives near Boston. He especially gravitated to his Aunt Nancy Bush Ellis in Lincoln, Massachusetts. He took some of

Watergate Scandal Explodes

In 1972, several undercover agents from the Republican Party tried to burglarize the Democratic National Headquarters in an apartment building called Watergate. They were indicted for this crime, but an elaborate cover-up followed to protect President Nixon, who denied any knowledge of the break-in. However, his own tapes revealed that he did know about the operation. Before Nixon could be impeached, he resigned in disgrace in August of 1974 and was succeeded by Vice President Gerald R. Ford. Because of this scandal the American public became disillusioned and distrustful of government and politicians. Watergate was particularly difficult for Bush because his father had been appointed chairman of the Republican National Committee by President Nixon.

his trusted friends to Kennebunkport or Greenwich on vacation breaks. Increasingly, he found Harvard restrictive. The Watergate scandal was widely discussed as the Vietnam War had been during his final year at Yale. Furthermore, he felt a self-imposed pressure to carry the Bush name forward into the next generation. When President Nixon resigned, there was some suggestion that Bush's father might become vice president for President Gerald R. Ford. Instead, President Ford appointed the elder Bush to be head of the U.S. Liaison Office to Communist China.

After graduating in 1975 from Harvard with a master's degree in business administration, life would take an unexpected turn for Bush.

SIX

Digging for Oil and Finding Romance

Before starting a business career, Bush spent six weeks in China visiting his parents. He thought it was a drab society. Everyone wore the same gray jackets and trousers. Free enterprise did not exist in China at this time. Bush's Harvard studies had only focused on life in an open, free, and colorful society. Communism under Chairman Mao was a shock to Bush.

Upon returning to American shores, Bush considered a trial run on Wall Street as a stockbroker. Instead, he drove to the wide-open spaces of Midland, Texas, where he had lived as a boy. He packed his blue Oldsmobile Cutlass with his belongings and headed to the hot, dusty Southwest much like his father had done years before after graduating from Yale.

LEARNING THE OIL BUSINESS

The oil business was booming, and Bush wanted to learn it inside out. He began as a land man. A land man's job is to research the ownership of mineral interests underneath the surface of a specific piece of land. The county courthouse was the place to find the deed records that contain this information.

Bush later became an oil prospector. He invested in a few holes, drilling for oil and gas. The first hole came up dry. The next one struck natural gas and Bush was able to pay his bills.

In Midland, Bush lived behind a couple's home in a one-room efficiency apartment. He was hardly ever there, except to sleep, and it was pretty messy. Despite his long hours working, he was lonely. So, he contacted old friends from elementary and junior high. Joe O'Neill, a bike-riding buddy, was one of those who had left Midland but returned because of the latest oil boom.

His renewed friendships included a couple of jogging buddies. Don Evans was one of them. His wife Susie had gone to elementary school with Bush. Charles Younger, an orthopedic surgeon, was the other part of the running trio. Younger, five years older than Bush, had lived diagonally across the street from the Bush family when they lived on West Ohio Street.

"When you run with people every day, you get to know them very well and how they think. When George wasn't a wise guy or calling us funny nicknames, I came to realize how sincere he was," said Younger. "I invested in his company because he was low risk. He didn't drill for oil like a wildcatter. He was cautious because he respected his investors. He assembled a team of loyal employees around him and was involved with their families. George was a casual sort of guy. He wore jeans, a tee shirt, and flip-flops. He had one blue suit. When he visited married couples for a good home-cooked meal, the wives did his laundry for him."

Coming back to Midland was like coming home for Bush. His childhood memories were still fresh. Many Texans feel a strong bond with each other. In fact, the meaning of the word *Texas* in Spanish (*Tejas*) is friends or friendship. Bush, like many Texans, made friends for life.

Another close friend was Karl C. Rove, who lived in Austin. Rove was born in Denver, Colorado, and moved to Utah with his parents. There he attended the University of Utah and later moved to Texas to enter politics. Rove would become a key political adviser to the elder Bush and eventually to George W.

On August 10, 1999, President-elect George W. Bush discusses his campaign plans with Karl C. Rove at the governor's mansion in Austin, Texas. Rove was his senior political strategist and a key member of Bush's "Iron Triangle." Karen Hughes and Joseph Allbaugh were the other two members of that triangle.

Bush often visited Rove in Austin and felt comfortable in his presence. Rove guided Bush's political reading to authors who disapproved of the 1960s. Marvin Olasky's *Tragedy of American Compassion*, David Horowitz's *Destructive Generation*, and Myron Magnet's *The Dream and The Nightmare* were some of the authors and books Rove recommended.

After a year as a land man, Bush started his own company. He worked hard, but he always made time for church. Bush attended the First Presbyterian Church on Sundays and volunteered to teach Sunday school as his father had done before him. There were fun times too, and girlfriends and plenty of Bush pranks.

A BRUSH WITH THE LAW

During his 1976 summer visit to Walker's Point in Maine, Bush was arrested for driving under the influence of alcohol. He was fined and his driver's license was suspended for one month. At the age of thirty, Bush was still worried about his father's reaction to this incident. His father called the police to thank them for doing their job with regard to his son. Any other reaction from his father was not mentioned.

Back in Texas, a political opportunity opened. Congressman Mahon from the Nineteenth Congressional District was about to resign. Don Evans suggested that Bush should run for that seat in 1977. His father, now head of the Central Intelligence Agency (CIA), was in favor of the idea too. Once again, Bush was moving along the path of tradition. His friends began to rally around him to help. Karl Rove was his political adviser, and Don Evans helped Rove in the management of the campaign. Joe O'Neill, a childhood friend, handled the money. Charles

Younger, though, thought it would be difficult for George to win against Democratic State Senator Kent Hance, who was well known in the area.

POLITICS AND ROMANCE

In the midst of the political battle, Jan and Joe O'Neill were trying to play cupid. For a long time, they had wanted to get Laura Welch to meet George W. Bush. Jan and Laura had been roommates at the Chateaux Dijon apartments in Houston when Laura was a second-grade teacher there.

Laura Welch had grown up in Midland as the only daughter of Jenna and Harold Welch, who was in the construction business. The Bushes and the Welches lived minutes away from each other, but never met. Although George W. and Laura went to different elementary schools, they were in the same junior high school.

From the time she was a child, Laura was quiet and always loved to read. Her mother, Jenna, had shared her own love of reading with her daughter. Laura's desire to become a teacher began in second grade. She adored her teacher, Charlene Gnagy, and wanted to be just like her. After school, Laura would set up her dolls in a row and play school, teaching them as Gnagy had taught her.

After Laura graduated from Midland Lee High School, she attended Southern Methodist University (SMU) located in an exclusive part of Dallas. She began her teaching career in Houston and later moved to Austin where she taught at a school attended by mostly Hispanic students. Then, she decided to study for a master's degree in library science at the University of Texas in Austin.

Throughout her college years, Laura had brought a number of young men home to meet her parents, but she had not found the right one. Jan O'Neill kept insisting that she should meet George, but Laura was not interested in politics and therefore, not interested in meeting him.

In August of 1977, she drove from Austin to Midland for the weekend to visit her parents. Jan telephoned her to ask if she would come to a

One of the greatest moments in Bush's life was his marriage to Laura Welch on November 5, 1977. The newlyweds pose outside the First United Methodist Church in Midland, Texas. From left to right: Marvin, Dorothy, Neil, Columba, Jeb, Laura, George W., Barbara, George Bush, and Dorothy Walker Bush.

barbecue and meet George. Reluctantly, she accepted. She did not expect to like him, but he talked and talked, making her laugh. Usually, when George went to the O'Neills for dinner, he would leave before nine. This time, he stayed until midnight.

The next day the foursome played miniature golf. Bush was smitten. He kept calling Laura in Austin and drove there to see her. At the end of August, he flew to Maine for a family gathering. Instead of staying for almost a week, he stayed only one day before flying back to Texas to see Laura. Barbara Bush suspected that her son was serious about this new young woman. She was right.

The young couple were engaged within three weeks and married within three months. Everyone was surprised because they were so different. Laura was quiet and reserved while George was outgoing. But they complemented each other perfectly. After George asked Harold Welch for his daughter's hand in marriage, he introduced Laura to his large family in Houston. They heartily approved.

George and Laura decided to have a quiet wedding in the chapel of Midland's First United Methodist Church, which had striking stained glass windows. Since both of them were thirty-one years old, they wanted a small wedding with only family and friends. Laura already had been a bridesmaid nine times for her friends. She didn't want anything elaborate. On November 5, 1977, Laura Welch and George W. Bush were married before a group of seventy-five people. After a short honeymoon in Mexico, the couple returned home to a little house that George had bought before their marriage.

George Bush for Congress

ON NOVEMBER 7,
VOTE FOR WEST TEXAS.
VOTE FOR
George Bush for Congress

Dear Voters,

Laura and I would like to take this opportunity to thank you for the many kindnesses you've shown us during my campaign for the Congress.

You've listened to me, and you've told me what you think. And hundreds of you have actively worked in my campaign.

I am very grateful to all of you.

During the past twelve months I have told you how much I want to represent you in the Congress. I mean that. I know I can do a good job.

Again, our thanks.

George W. Bush

This was a 1978 campaign poster when Bush was running for Congress in West Texas. He and Laura posed together. Bush lost.

SEVEN

A New Family and Big Time Politics

After the honeymoon was over, the newlyweds hit the campaign trail from the final month of 1977 to November of 1978. They covered the Nineteenth Congressional District from end to end. Laura dreaded giving speeches in George's place. Still, everything seemed to be going well. Even though Texas folks knew George W. was eastern born and had gone to Yale and Harvard, they accepted him because he had Texas in his bones. On election night, though, George W. Bush lost his first political race, as his friend Charles Younger had predicted he might.

Years before, his father had lost a senate race in Houston. With this knowledge as some comfort, George W. went back to the oil fields to work. He decided to give up the job as land man and start his own company, which he called Arbusto. In Spanish, *Arbusto* means "shrub" or "bush." The name was subject to endless ridicule among the seasoned oil men. When many of his oil drillings came up empty, the rivals laughed even more, shouting "A bust oh!" Eventually, George changed the company name to Bush Exploration.

Meanwhile, the elder George Bush had sought the Republican nomination for president of the United States in 1980 and had fallen short. But he made a strong enough showing that Ronald Reagan, the Republican winner, asked him to be his running mate. The Reagan-Bush team won against Democrat Jimmy Carter.

Only a few months into the Reagan presidency, there was an assassination attempt on President Ronald Reagan. After he made a speech at a Washington Hotel on March 30, 1981, he walked to his car. Before stepping into his limousine, someone shot at Reagan. Reagan's bodyguard shoved the wounded president into the limousine and headed for the nearest hospital. The Secret Service men tackled and handcuffed the young man with the gun, John Hinckley, Jr., who was suffering from a mental illness.

The bullet had barely missed the president's heart, and it became lodged in his lung. Always a man of humor, Reagan told his wife, "Honey, I forgot to duck." Before the doctors started to operate on him, he said to them, "I hope all of you are Republicans!"

When George W. Bush heard the news about Ronald Reagan, he was alarmed because any mishap to Reagan might mean that his father would step into the presidency. The elder Bush was in an airplane at the time of the shooting, but the airplane immediately changed course to return to Washington. George W. Bush was a great admirer of Ronald Reagan and his politics. Bush's father was a loyal political partner to Reagan. To everyone's relief, Ronald Reagan recovered and resumed his duties.

STARTING A FAMILY

Since their marriage in 1977, Laura and George had wanted to have a family. But after several years of not being able to conceive children, they decided to adopt. The day before they were to sign the adoption papers, Laura discovered that she was pregnant. The doctor told the happy couple that they would be the parents of twin girls. Laura and George were ecstatic. George sent his wife two-dozen red roses upon hearing the news.

The pregnancy was not easy. Laura developed toxemia. Toxemia in pregnancy produces high-blood pressure, weakness in the muscles, and swelling. The only cure was complete bed rest. She couldn't travel to Maine or do anything strenuous. The doctor sent her to the hospital

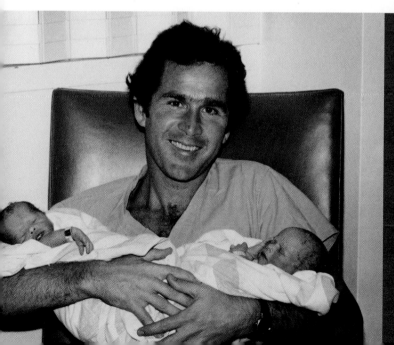

George Bush was an involved father. Here, he holds his twin daughters, Barbara and Jenna, born in November of 1981. He walked the floors, singing Yale football songs, to stop the babies from crying.

about seven weeks before the babies were due. The parents decided to go to a Dallas hospital instead of one in Midland or Houston. If the doctor hadn't delivered the babies on November 25, 1981, Laura's kidneys were in danger of failing. The little girls weighed no more than four to five pounds each. They were named Jenna Welch Bush and Barbara Pierce Bush after their grandmothers.

The thrilled parents took their twin babies home to Midland. Like many new parents, they were unprepared for parenthood and couldn't understand why the babies cried so much. They tried everything to comfort the babies. George W. was an involved father. He changed diapers and walked the floors with one baby in each arm. He marched around their house singing Yale football songs: "Bulldog, Bulldog, bow wow wow." Today, when the twins see photos of their father holding them and singing, they collapse into gales of laughter.

Six months after the twins were born, Reverend Charles Lutrick baptized them. "I invited the senior Bushes to attend, but they declined because they wanted the babies to be the focus of attention. On that very day, George W. Bush joined the First United Methodist Church in Midland," said Lutrick. "George taught adult classes and helped Laura with young adult classes. They attended the 'Wednesday Night Live' fellowship gatherings, too. Shortly before the family moved to Washington, Bush was appointed chairman of the church's finance board."

By 1983, Bush Exploration had merged with a company called Spectrum Seven. Bush was paid a very good salary and given 1.1 million shares of stock. Unfortunately, Spectrum Seven began losing money because of a sinking stock market and lower oil prices. Bush agreed to let Harken Energy of Dallas buy the company. Harken then put Bush on its board of directors as a salaried consultant.

TWO LIFE-CHANGING EXPERIENCES

Two experiences changed George W. Bush's life. In 1985, he was visiting at the family house in Kennebunkport, Maine. The evangelist minister Billy Graham had befriended and counseled many presidents on spiritual

Billy Graham has been a spirtual advisor and friend to the Bush family for many years. He is pictured here standing between Laura and George Bush.

matters over the years. He was spending a weekend with the Bushes at Walker's Point. One evening after dinner, everyone was gathered in the living room discussing a variety of topics when the conversation turned to spiritual questions. Although Bush cannot point to anything specific during the discussion, he felt great compassion and love from Billy Graham. Something about the man and the events of that evening seemed to stir Bush's soul.

When Bush returned to Midland, he discussed this spiritual awakening with his good friend Don Evans. Evans attended a weekly men's Bible group sponsored by the Methodist Church and invited Bush to come. Although Bush already read the Bible daily, he found that this Bible group opened a whole new dimension in his life.

The second experience happened in May of 1986. Three couples—the O'Neills, the Evanses, and the Bushes—from Midland decided to celebrate their fortieth birthdays together. They chose the Broadmoor Hotel in Colorado Springs with its breathtaking views of Pikes Peak. They planned to play golf, jog, and party. Neil Bush had come over from Denver to celebrate with them. The partying went on much too late.

When morning came, Bush intended to take his usual early morning jog. Upon awakening, he felt terrible. His head ached, and his body didn't want to move. At that moment, he told Laura he was going to stop drinking. Laura had encouraged him to make that decision many times before. From that time, Bush never took another drink. His mind became clear and his body became fit so that he could keep running. A few years later, he decided to stop smoking. Once these decisions were made, he never turned back to those old ways.

GETTING DAD ELECTED

Grooming his father for the presidential election in 1988 was the next order of business for Bush. It was the right time to move his family to the heart of the beltway in Washington, D.C., to work toward that possibility.

During the final days of his vice presidency, the elder Bush and his son worked closely together as political strategists. The two families enjoyed a closeness too. Throughout the whirlwind of campaigning, George W. was the defender and protector of his father. He bristled at any criticism of his father and would chastise the reporters openly for any critical comments.

George H. W. Bush defeated his Democratic opponent, Michael Dukakis and was sworn into office as the forty-first president of the United States in January of 1989. George W. Bush had the satisfaction of knowing that his father had finally succeeded in his lifelong goal and that he had helped make it happen. It was time for the first son and his family to return to Texas.

In August of 1988, young George Bush campaigned hard for his father's presidential bid. The elder Bush defeated Democratic contender, Michael Dukakis, on election night.

EIGHT

Bush's Dream Baseball Deal

Before trading in the exciting Washington life for a return to Texas, Bush was constantly on the telephone with Midland's Eddie Chiles, a rich oil man who owned the Texas Rangers baseball team based in Arlington, a suburb of Dallas. A friend had told Bush that the ball club was for sale for $80 million. The money was way too much for Bush to afford, but he put his organizational skills to work. If he could patch together a group of investors, it might work. Bush telephoned everyone he knew around the country—and even some people he did not know well—soliciting part owners.

Finally, Bush did it. With loans for his own $600,000 share and the rest of the money from other investors, ownership of the Texas Rangers looked possible. However, it was pointed out to Bush that he didn't have enough investors from Texas. Eddie Chiles steered him to two multimillionaires to clinch the final partnership. Rusty Rose from Dallas was one of them. Bush owned 1.8 percent of the team.

Because baseball had been Bush's obsession since his Little League days in Midland, he felt a dream had come true. After all, it was in his blood. His great-uncle, George Herbert Walker, had been a majority owner of the New York Mets. His uncle once introduced him to Casey Stengel, who managed the Yankees for seven championships. As new owners of the Texas Rangers, George and Laura were entitled to a private

Bush's pride and joy was his part ownership in the Texas Rangers baseball team. Here, the Rangers played against the Baltimore Orioles in April 1998 at the new stadium in Arlington, Texas.

box above the stands. Instead, they chose to sit on the front row right next to the team's dugout. Bush liked hanging around the practices, chatting with players such as pitcher Nolan Ryan.

One of the things Bush had learned at Harvard Business School was how to delegate. He and Rusty Rose let the baseball experts run the team while he and Rose managed the business part. In a way, it was similar to politics. Speeches and fundraisers by Bush brought fans and families to the bleachers of the ball field. His publicity efforts paid off because the stands were full at most games.

"George loves people and baseball, so he traveled to all 254 counties in Texas, promoting the Texas Rangers," said his friend Dr. Charles Younger from Midland. " I think owning the Texas Rangers was his happiest time in life. And going to all those counties was good preparation for his future political career."

According to Laura's mother, Jenna Welch, the family loved going to the games, sitting right next to the dugout while the twins had fun running around. Family and friends also enjoyed eating at the private Rangers Club.

Bush was part of an effort to build a new stadium for $189 million. He and Rose devised a plan whereby the city of Arlington would pay half, and private donations would pay the rest. Today the red-brick, fortresslike stadium sits amid roller coasters and beautiful landscaping. The walls of the building have carved friezes, showing the history of Texas. All around the building above the friezes, there are the heads of Longhorn cattle and Lone Stars made from cast-stone. Outside, the Texas and American flags ripple in the wind.

In 1990 the buzz around Texas was that Bush might run for governor, but Democrat Ann Richards was a strong candidate. Richards had made a savage remark about the elder Bush during the 1988 presidential campaign. At the Democratic convention, Richards had said, "Poor George, he can't help it. . . . He was born with a silver foot in his mouth." The whole Bush family was deeply offended as they watched Richards on television.

When Barbara Bush was asked if her son might run for governor of Texas in 1990, she said she was opposed to it. George W. himself had no intention of running. For one thing, he was involved with the Texas

Iraq Invades Kuwait

In the Middle East, Iraq and its leader, Saddam Hussein, a one-time friend of the United States, invaded its tiny neighbor Kuwait, hoping to seize its oil fields. Kuwait asked the United States to come to its aid. The United Nations denounced the Iraqi action. A coalition of thirty countries led by the United States assembled 800,000 troops under the direction of U.S. General H. Norman Schwarzkopf. President Bush gave Iraq until January 15, 1991, to pull out of Kuwait. When they refused, Operation Desert Shield began with daily bombings of Iraq's elite Republican Guard. On February 23, 1991, George Bush gave the signal for the ground troop campaign, called Desert Storm, to begin. Within one hundred hours, the Iraqi army had been driven from Kuwait, and President Bush called off the war. Twelve U.N. resolutions prevented the coalition from invading Iraq. The handling of the Persian Gulf War made President George H. W. Bush very popular.

Rangers. He also sensed this wasn't the right time. Besides, the family was happy in Dallas, and the twins liked their school. Ann Richards won the election and took office in 1991.

BLACK SHEEP OF THE FAMILY

In May of 1992, George and Laura were invited to the White House during the visit of Great Britain's Queen Elizabeth II. At luncheon, Barbara Bush put her first son at the end of the table. The queen wondered why he was banished to this far place. In her book, *Barbara Bush: A Memoir*, Bush's mother related the following anecdote.

"He's the black sheep of the family," replied Barbara.

"Every family has one," said George W. "Who is the one in your family?" The queen laughed with a merry twinkle in her eye and said, "None of your business." The queen turned to Barbara Bush and asked what her son had done to qualify him as the black sheep. Barbara answered that her son said exactly what he thought and wore cowboy boots with God Bless America on them.

Then, the queen asked the first son if he planned to wear boots to the formal state dinner that evening. "Yes," said George W. "But they will say, 'God Save the Queen.'" The queen seemed amused and delighted by the humor of the forthright son.

Meanwhile, there were challenges to the elder Bush's reelection in 1992. The economy had slumped after the Persian Gulf War. Ross Perot, a Texas billionaire, captured the imagination of the American public as an independent candidate. He spent $4 million of his own money to put his name on the ballots in all fifty states. A right-wing Republican, Pat

The two Georges, father and son, stroll casually on the south lawn driveway of the White House in April of 1992. Little did the son realize that nine years later, he would become president of the United States.

Buchanan, also launched his campaign. These two candidates split the Republican vote three ways, damaging incumbent George H. W. Bush's chances.

Added to these complications was the Democratic candidate from Arkansas, Governor Bill Clinton. Young and attractive, Clinton capitalized on the splintered Republican Party and focused on the economy, which was recovering slowly.

After President Bush was defeated by Bill Clinton in the presidential election, he and Barbara returned to Houston to live. Laura and George resumed their Dallas life with their twins and the baseball team. It was a sad time for all the Bushes.

Shortly after his return, George W. decided to train for a marathon race. Every day he ran through the neighborhood streets of Dallas and on a track near his home. When Bush ran in the Houston marathon, his parents cheered when their first son finished the race in three hours and forty-four minutes. Following the marathon, Bush made a decision to run another kind of race.

NINE

A Home Run for the Governor

In 1992, only a few weeks after the Bushes left the White House the news came that Dorothy Walker Bush had died in Greenwich, Connecticut, at the family homestead. She was ninety-one years old. Relatives all gathered for the final good-bye. Dorothy had been the family matriarch who had preached good manners, fair play, and a competitive spirit to her children and grandchildren.

Back in Texas, George W. Bush decided to test the political waters again. He campaigned for his Camp Longhorn friend Kay Bailey Hutchison, who was running for U.S. senator from Texas—a race she won. Along the way, people kept asking Bush if he were going to run for governor against Ann Richards in 1994. He would not answer directly, but indicated his interest.

A RUN FOR GOVERNOR

Meanwhile, political polls conducted by Karl Rove in Texas showed that Ann Richards had a 58 percent approval rating. Although she was a colorful candidate with some witty one-liners and Texas-style stories, some politicians figured that her first election had been a result of the public's dislike of her Republican opponent Clayton Williams. Nevertheless, Richards was a strong governor. In her four years, she improved the image of Texas throughout the rest of the country. Company scandals that arose from bad loans and crooked business deals in the 1980s had damaged the state's reputation. She wanted to reshape the "New Texas." Richards also brought in a group of technology companies from California, providing

Middle East Peace Signing

In the world at large, peace efforts in the Middle East seemed to be working during this era. In 1993, President Bill Clinton brought Prime Minister Yitzhak Rabin of Israel, his foreign minister Shimon Peres, and Chairman Yasser Arafat, leader of the Palestinians, to the peace table. On the White House lawn, the leaders shook hands and signed a peace document based on the earlier Oslo Peace Accords. Rabin, Arafat, and Peres would be awarded the Nobel Peace Prize in 1994 for the efforts to bring an end to the conflict between Israel and the Palestinians. Unfortunately, Rabin was assassinated in November of 1995 by an Israeli law student, and the peace process was set back for years.

more employment for Texans. Her popularity was particularly strong with African Americans and Hispanics.

However, the Republican strategists thought that Bush had a good chance of beating Richards in the 1994 election, especially after Kay Bailey Hutchison won the senate race as a Republican. Barbara Bush, though, was convinced Ann Richards couldn't be beaten by her son.

While Bush and Rove were determining how the political winds were blowing in Texas, Jeb Bush was running for governor of Florida. Many believed that his political future was brighter than his older brother's. Jeb was a Phi Beta Kappa graduate of the University of Texas and was a bright, quiet, and thoughtful young man. When asked if his

In 1994, Bush begins his own campaign for governor of Texas. He gathers support in Houston.

younger brother were more intelligent, George W. Bush humorously replied, "I'm smarter. He's the tall one."

Back in the Lone Star state, George was campaigning east and west and north and south. There were four messages that he hammered over and over: education, juvenile justice, tort reform (preventing people from demanding large sums of money from businesses in lawsuits for accidents and injuries), and welfare reform. Sensing that Bush might enter the race, the Texas Democrats weren't worried because they thought he would self-destruct by losing his temper in the campaign. Any time his father was criticized, Bush would get angry and lash out at reporters. The Democrats were sure Bush would lose his cool and wouldn't last.

Bush surprised the Democrats by making a clear distinction between defending his father and being a candidate himself. From his point of view, if someone you love is criticized, you react differently. When you are the one being criticized, it's not a big deal. Criticism didn't seem to bother Bush. Experience had toughened him. By admitting to his slightly wild and immature behavior as a young man at the beginning of the race, he put himself in an underdog position and helped to stop the rumors circulating about him.

Richards responded to her new opponent by delivering stinging jabs in her usual style. Some of the names she called him were "jerk" and "shrub." Her attacks backfired. People laughed, but they didn't like the name-calling. Bush stayed focused on the issues and refused to lash back at her. He didn't want anything negative he said against her to be misinterpreted as revenge for the "silver foot" comment she had made about his father. Because Bush took the high ground and dealt with Texas concerns rather than personality, the Dallas and Houston newspapers endorsed him in their editorials, favoring his stand on issues.

By the time election night came in November of 1994, George Bush had a strong lead. It hadn't been easy. In September Richards' lead was 60 percent. He had two months to catch up to her. He did. By 10:00 P.M. on election night, Richards called Bush to concede the election. He had won by a slight margin of 54 percent to 45 percent. It was a sweet victory celebrated by George, Laura, and the twins at an Austin hotel. Despite Jeb's election loss in the race for Florida governor, the Bush family was excited for their first son's victory in Texas.

After the election results, George and Laura sold their Dallas home to move with the twins into the governor's mansion in Austin, the capital of Texas. The mansion is a beautiful white-pillared Greek Revival style home where Texas governors have lived since 1856. It stands on a green lawn amid trees and fragrant bushes, enclosed by a wrought iron fence. It is located right across the street from the capitol building.

Austin has a special charm. The capitol dome, with its goddess of liberty holding the Lone Star on top, is silhouetted against the Texas sky at dawn and dusk. Austin is a lively city with many ethnic restaurants and hordes of young people from the University of Texas. Politicians huddle and deal at the Texas Chili Parlor or the Austin Club. Affluent residents live among the rolling hills of the western suburbs. Town Lake, with miles of hiking and biking trails along its banks, where the new governor would jog, is formed by the Colorado River as it flows through the city. Also, Austin is known as the "live music" capital of the country because of its vibrant music scene.

An aerial view shows the rose-granite state house and grounds in Austin, Texas, where George W. Bush would officiate as Republican governor from 1994 to 2000.

Bush had to move into the high-ceilinged office at the rose-granite state capitol building and prove that he could govern. He hired his old classmate from Andover and Yale, Clay Johnson, to handle the many appointments the new governor had to make. Johnson was a successful businessman, not a politician, and Bush trusted him completely. Johnson could tell whether someone was interested in serving the governor or more interested in his or her own personal ambition. He would later assume this role at the White House.

The Texas house and senate meet only once every two years for 140 days. So, preparation for bills has to take place in the year between the sessions. Those 150 house members and 31 senators have to consider each bill. They are consulted and courted by both parties.

The senate and house chambers have an old-world elegance about them. The chandeliers are shaped like a Lone Star with the letters of Texas in between the points of the star. There are soft, tan leather chairs for the members and telephones tucked under the leg of each desk. Microphones fit into the holes that once held ink bottles.

Clay Johnson, a trusted friend, has worked for Bush for many years. He would later serve as the Bush-Cheney transition director when Bush became president.

BUSH-CHENEY
TRANSITION

Against this background of Texas politics, Bush faced an uphill battle. His task was to become bipartisan and win over some Democrats if he wanted to get anything done in the legislature. The first man he had to persuade was Lieutenant Governor Bob Bullock, a veteran politician of forty years. Bullock was a slightly built man whose chiseled face resembled that of a figure on Mount Rushmore. He wielded tremendous power in Texas and would not make a good enemy.

As the new governor, Bush drove to Bullock's home in west Austin to call on him. George told the granite-faced Democrat that he wanted to work with him and get things done because it was right for Texas. Bullock wasn't won over, but he was interested enough in the bold strategy to meet Bush halfway.

George Bush shares a humorous moment with the tough Democratic Lt. Governor of Texas, Bob Bullock. They are beginning the first day of the legislative session in 1999 at the state capital in Austin.

A GOVERNOR OF ACTION

One of Bush's first actions was to schedule a weekly breakfast meeting with Bullock and Pete Laney, the speaker of the house. The trio rotated their meetings among their three offices. Bush and Bullock were tough negotiators, but there was laughter too. Bullock could spin a lot of rich and raw Texas stories. During many of those sessions, Bush just listened.

Bush wanted to fulfill his campaign promise on tort reform. Lawsuits took much more money from businesses than the actual damages cost. Bush tried to get Bullock to put a reasonable cap on these damages. Bullock wanted $1 million, but Bush resisted. They compromised at $750,000.

However, Bush's most important reform was in education. Bush thought the public school system needed to be reshaped. By 1995, the legislature had passed most of his specific goals. Bush wanted to be sure that credit for the changes was given to the hardworking legislature. Giving credit to others was another family trait from the house of Bush.

PICNICS AND POLITICS

After his first one hundred days in office, Bush invited everyone to the governor's mansion for a picnic. He was aware that social contacts with the Democrats were as important as with the Republicans. In fact, throughout his working day, Bush would wander through the rotunda, stride up and down the shiny granite halls, shake hands, and visit with legislators. Casually, he would drop into his opponents' offices for a chat. Socializing made cooperation easier, and Bush was good at these friendly encounters.

As the first lady of Texas, Laura Bush launched the state's first Book Fair Festival on the premises of the capitol. Talks by authors were delivered in both the senate and house chambers. The affair raised over $900,000 for libraries in Texas. Also, to show their support for Texas education, the Bushes sent their daughters to public high school. Both girls graduated from Austin High School in 2000.

During his time as governor, Bush and his family grew closer to the Bullocks. Bullock even deserted his own party to back Bush for his reelection as governor in 1998. This was considered the ultimate betrayal by the Texas Democratic Party. He also told the elder Bush that his son should be president.

Like a Son

Bob Bullock became very ill in 1999. While Bush was campaigning for the presidency, he received a telephone call, warning of Bullock's impending death. He and Laura flew back to Austin to see their friend. The two men asked to be left alone. They cried together. And then, Bullock asked Bush to give the eulogy at his funeral. He had come to look upon Bush as his son. It was a sad time when the tough, old politician died. Now, the Bob Bullock Museum, depicting the history of Texas, honors the veteran political warrior.

KEEPING CAMPAIGN PROMISES

As Bush moved through his term as governor, he continued to work on the campaign promises he had made. In 1995, he began to reform the juvenile justice system. Instead of letting young people in prison sit and do nothing, there were programs to provide exercise for them and jobs created for them inside the prison walls. Even study initiatives were designed for their benefit. If churches had effective drug and alcohol programs for young people and couldn't fund them, Bush announced a "faith-based program" to let them continue with financial support from the state. This program was adopted in 1997 and again in 1999.

Improving Texas education was one of Bush's priorities. Reading was strongly emphasized in the Bush plan. In 1996, the public school curriculum made sure students really could read at grade level by third grade. It is thought that the phrase, "no child left behind," originated in this period. A child who couldn't read was not to be ignored or forgotten, but must be helped. Educators supported this philosophy, but an unpopular initiative for many of them was the regular testing of teachers.

However, one of the toughest decisions George W. Bush had to make as governor was carrying out the death penalty on a high profile case in 1998. Karla Faye Tucker had been on death row in Texas for thirteen years. Years before, Tucker and her boyfriend, under the influence of drugs, had brutally murdered a young man and woman. At the time of the trial, Tucker showed no remorse. Shortly after Tucker's imprisonment, she had a religious conversion and asked forgiveness for her misdeeds. Over the years, Tucker helped many young women change their lives in prison by introducing them to Christianity.

With regard to the death penalty, a Texas governor is guided by the recommendation from the Texas Board of Pardons and Paroles. If any new evidence from the crime is found in the prisoner's favor, a stay of execution for thirty days is allowed. In Tucker's case, nothing new was found. Despite her spiritual transformation, the facts about the murders had not changed. Governor Bush had to abide by Texas law and follow through with the execution even though national publicity surrounded the case and there was a lot of sympathy for Tucker. His final words were, "May God bless Karla Faye Tucker and the victims and their families."

While Bush tackled difficult issues as governor, there was talk of him running for a higher office. Rumors at the Republican National Convention in 1996 were that George W. Bush might be the candidate for president of the United States in the 2000 election. By 1997, these rumors had become a reality.

The beginning of the twenty-first century would bring an American political dynasty not seen since the days of John Adams and his son, John Quincy Adams. The Bush family did not like talk of a dynasty. Bush said that in a dynasty one was given everything, but that in a democracy everything had to be earned. He dismissed the idea, but the public liked the historical comparison with the Adams dynasty.

Making History as President

A gradual political movement began in 1997 to bring George W. Bush's name to Republicans and to the country as a presidential candidate. Strategist Karl Rove mapped out the plan quietly behind the scenes in Austin.

At the same time, Bush was planning to run for a second term as Texas governor. In December of 1997, he made a special appearance at his own Sam Houston Elementary School in Midland to speak to the children and make his official announcement about a second term for governor of Texas. If he failed in his run for the presidency, he would still have a job.

In Bush's 1998 quest for reelection in Texas, he won by a landslide of 70 percent of the votes, including 50 percent of the Hispanic vote. This was the first time a Republican governor had won two consecutive terms in Texas. His brother Jeb also won his first-term election for governor of Florida on his second try. Many from the Bush clan attended two inaugurations: one in Tallahassee, Florida, and the other in Austin, Texas. It was a proud moment for George and Barbara Bush.

Oklahoma City Bombing

While Bush served his first term as governor, a bombing attack in Oklahoma City shocked people everywhere. On the morning of April 19, 1995, government workers were arriving for work at the Murrah Federal Building in downtown Oklahoma City. Some were taking their children to daycare in the same building. Just before 9:00 A.M. an explosion ripped through the building, turning it into twisted rubble and killing 168 adults and children. The city and the nation were stunned and horrified. A young American, Timothy McVeigh, was soon arrested. He had left explosives in a rental truck to blow up the building. Terry McNichols was arrested as his accomplice.

Apparently McVeigh was angry at the U.S. government for its part in the Persian Gulf War, where McVeigh had served in the army. He also resented the FBI for its role in the deaths of people at the Branch Davidian compound in Waco, Texas, a few years earlier. McVeigh was tried, convicted, and sentenced for the crime. He was executed by lethal injection on June 11, 2001.

While George W. Bush was working with the 1999 Texas legislature from January to June, pressing for better education and tax cuts, a powerful trio was preparing presidential plans for him. They were Karl Rove as his chief political strategist, Karen Hughes as spokesperson and media relations person, and Joe Allbaugh as campaign manager. Of the three, Rove had the most influence. Midland friend, Don Evans had an important role as a fundraiser.

In 1999, a former Bush president sits between two Bush governors—George W. of Texas and Jeb of Florida. They share a family joke.

GETTING READY TO RUN

Karen Hughes developed a coaching plan for her boss. She brought experts in foreign policy, economics, and education to the governor's office, the governor's mansion, or the Austin Club. The purpose was to build Bush's knowledge of global and national affairs. The Texas governor announced the formation of an exploratory committee in 1999 to test the waters regarding his chances as a Republican candidate. One part of the election

Press spokeswoman, Karen Hughes, offers final words of advice to her boss, Governor George Bush, before a press conference outside the governor's mansion on November 8, 2000.

process that Bush didn't like was the intense examination of his personality by the media. He called it "psychobabble."

In April of 1998, Governor Bush went to San Francisco to give a talk at a Republican fund-raising dinner. The next day, Bush visited Stanford University where George P. Shultz, secretary of state for Ronald Reagan, invited Bush to come to his home on campus in between his commitments. Shultz, a Distinguished Fellow at the Hoover Institute at Stanford, gathered a group of renowned economists and former public servants to spend an hour or two (which turned into four hours) with the young Bush. Condoleezza Rice, Provost of Stanford University, was there too. Bush and Rice, who had met briefly before, had an immediate rapport, according to Shultz.

"We talked policy—foreign and economic," said Shultz. "He argued with us, held his own, and enjoyed it. We were impressed by his questions. Usually, someone asks one question and then dries up on the subject. Governor Bush came back again and again. He knew how to dig in. I suggested that he should run for president because he seemed to have a real grasp of things."

"I thought his reply was interesting," commented Mr. Shultz. "Governor Bush said there were two things that would influence his decision. One was his family—the impact on his daughters. And the other was to convince himself what he could get accomplished as president."

Shultz further noted, "President Bush has the capacity to make sound decisions. He is underestimated as president because many people in Washington consider him an outsider. He is just himself. Furthermore, he has a strong character. Both he and his appealing wife set a moral tone."

HOME ON THE RANGE

With the pressure of campaigning ahead of them, George and Laura decided they wanted a private retreat in central Texas. They found 1,600 acres (647.5 ha) of rich, dark soil near Crawford, Texas. The Albrecht

On September 18, 2000, Laura and George Bush retreat to their Crawford, Texas, ranch after campaigning for Bush's bid for the presidency. Their faithful dog, Spot, trots along beside them.

family had owned the lush green land, raising crops, cattle, and horses. George and Laura were enchanted by seven canyons, a grotto, the Bosque River, Bluff Creek, and a wash over Rainey's Creek on the property. Bush could see himself driving over this land in a four-wheel-drive pickup truck. They decided to buy it and hired the previous owner's son, Kenneth Albrecht, to manage it.

The ranch would not be fancy. Among a grove of oak and pecan trees overlooking a lake, they had their own house built from glass and local limestone. It included a geothermal heating system. There were views in every direction from the porches. They added a guest house for visitors and planned to plant buffalo grass. From town, the ranch is a little more than 7 miles (11 km) on a paved yellow road. When the grass along the road is tall and jade green, the ranch can't be seen by those who pass by.

The town of Crawford, with a population of seven hundred people, has a gas station, a post office, a barbershop, and a little cafe that serves cheesecake, buttermilk pie, and rancher's pie. No one there was prepared for a large tourist invasion.

As the national campaign intensified, Bush had some hurdles to overcome. The media pressed him about his knowledge of foreign affairs. When Pakistan was taken over by a general who became president, a Boston TV reporter asked Bush about him. Bush couldn't pronounce the name of Pervez Musharraf and other leaders in the region. As a result, the press pounced on his fumblings and called him an intellectual lightweight compared to his more experienced opponent Al Gore.

However, Bush's main opponent within the Republican Party was Senator John McCain, who was gaining popularity. McCain's heroism as a prisoner of war for seven years in North Vietnam and his attacks on campaign financing were appealing to the public. Furthermore, McCain got along well with the press. He was always open to interviews, and this certainly made him popular among the media.

Only days before the New Hampshire primary in 2000, voters were questioning whether Bush was ready to become president. John McCain won that primary. It was a blow to the Bush camp. Bush recovered by winning the primary in South Carolina. After that, McCain could never regain his momentum.

Before the Republican National Convention assembled in Philadelphia, Bush selected Dick Cheney for his vice presidential running mate. Cheney had been his father's secretary of defense and was

Dick Cheney, former secretary of defense under President George H.W. Bush, is named George W. Bush's running mate as vice president for the 2000 presidential election.

well-informed about global issues. The delegates at the convention backed the team. Laura Bush also gave a simple, heartwarming speech that introduced her to the American public. In the beginning, Laura wasn't sure if she wanted her husband to run for president because of the criticism that would be directed at him and the family. But she knew her husband had a mission.

Once the two political conventions were over, Democrat Al Gore and Republican George Bush traveled around the country with their campaign messages. Gore had selected Senator Joseph Lieberman from Connecticut for his running mate, making Lieberman the first Jewish vice presidential candidate. The differences between the two presidential hopefuls were not extreme. Both Bush and Gore were from prominent and wealthy families and had advanced degrees. However, Gore had more experience in government, as a senator from Tennessee and as Bill Clinton's vice president for eight years. Bush was only entering his second term as Texas governor. Both candidates were for lower prices on prescription drugs for seniors. They both wanted to save Social Security. Education was also a major concern of both.

However, Gore was more liberal on all of these social issues than Bush. Bush knew he had to bring the Christian Right into his camp as well as other groups of Republican conservatives. On the issue of abortion, Bush was pro-life and Gore pro-choice. Political analyst Dick Morris concluded that if Gore had not given the impression of arrogance and pushiness during the televised debates and had promoted environmental issues (on which he is an expert), he could have won the election.

BUSH ALMOST DERAILED

Throughout the three debates against his Democratic opponent, Bush gave a better showing than expected. Momentum was gaining for the Texan. Then, only days before voting at the polls, Bush's 1976 drunk driving citation in Maine was uncovered, causing a media frenzy. When faced by this revelation, Bush admitted it. The reason for his silence on

Presidential hopeful, Governor George Bush, awaits the election results in Austin, Texas, on November 7, 2000. His wife Laura along with his mother and father wait with him. The election results would not be settled until thirty-six days later.

the drunk driving charge for so many years, he explained, was to shield his teenage daughters from knowing about his misbehavior.

Over the months of the campaign, George Bush stressed several themes. He wanted to improve education so that "no child was left behind." He floated the idea of tax cuts. Calling himself a "compassionate conservative," he hoped to attract moderates and independents. He also advocated a strong military while Gore was against increased defense spending.

On election night, November 7, 2000, members of the Bush family waited for the results in a suite at the Four Seasons Hotel in Austin. Early in the evening, newscasters projected that Al Gore had won in Florida. That announcement was later withdrawn because the panhandle of Florida had not yet counted its votes. Things became tense. Then, the election seemed to swing to Bush by midnight. Al Gore made a concession call to Bush, but called him back two hours later to retract the concession. The election was too close to call.

Apparently there was a problem in Florida where Jeb Bush was governor. Senior citizens in Palm Beach, Miami-Dade, and Broward counties had been confused by the way the ballot was arranged and said they punched the wrong holes when they voted.

MAKING ELECTION HISTORY

This was the beginning of political fireworks. The public had to wait another thirty-six days to know whom their new president would be. The counting and recounting were not satisfactory. Lawsuits were brought by both sides. Both candidates hired the best lawyers in the country to defend them. Finally, the case moved from the circuit court to the Florida Supreme Court and finally to the United States Supreme Court. There the vote was close—five to four in favor of Bush. On December 12, 2000, the highest court in the land declared that George W. Bush was the winner with 271 electoral votes as opposed to 267 for Al Gore. The public was relieved to have a resolution. Al Gore, of course, was disappointed and George Bush was cautiously pleased. Bush made his acceptance speech in the house chamber of the Texas capitol in Austin.

This election of the forty-third president was historic for the United States. Not since John Adams became the country's second president in 1797 and his son, John Quincy Adams, became the sixth president in 1825, had another father and son both won the presidency. But there were other similarities as well. Both the Adamses and the Bushes had roots in New England. Men in both families graduated from famous universities. Both families had a high sense of ethics and believed strongly in service to their country. The fathers of the first sons wrote long and frequent letters to their wives, children, and friends, leaving a full record of their historic lives. Unlike the Adams men, however, the Bush men were openly sentimental. Jeb Bush has said, "The Bush men cry a lot."

George H. W. Bush took office in 1993 as the forty-first president. The first son followed in his father's footsteps in January of 2001 to become the forty-third president. At the George H. W. Bush Presidential Library, in College Station, Texas, at the Texas A & M University, are exhibits about John Adams and John Quincy Adams. Other areas depict the presidential lives of the two Bushes. "Two families and four presidents" is the quote at the entrance to the Adams and Bush rooms.

Once George W. Bush knew he was officially elected president, he began announcing his cabinet. The appointment of General Colin Powell as his secretary of state was not a surprise. Condoleezza Rice, an African American woman of tremendous intellect who had outstanding qualifications, was nominated as national security adviser. Bush's longtime

After the inauguration in January of 2001, President and Mrs. Bush walk in the rain to the White House.

friend Don Evans was tapped for secretary of commerce. New Jersey Governor Christine Todd Whitman was named head of the Environmental Protection Agency (EPA). The cabinet team was a strong one.

On their way to the inauguration ceremonies in Washington, George and Laura Bush stopped in Midland, Texas, for a large celebration. Then, on January 29, 2001, before the world and his immediate family, George W. Bush was sworn into office as the forty-third president of the United States.

When the inaugural celebration was over, the Bush twins returned to their freshman year in college—Barbara at Yale and Jenna at the University of Texas, George and Laura Bush settled into the White House private quarters with their two dogs and one cat.

FACING CHALLENGES

President Bush took the reins of government. Almost immediately, he introduced his Texas program, the Faith-Based Initiative to help prisoners and youth with problems relating to drugs and alcohol. For the Department of Education, he recommended an 11 percent increase in the budget. In February of 2001, he recommended a $21 billion increase in Medicare. Also in February, Bush met with Vincente Fox, president of Mexico, to discuss controlling immigration on the border between Mexico and the United States. In early April, he attended a summit meeting of all the countries in the Americas.

The first real test of his presidential ability came on April 9, 2001, when a Chinese jet fighter threatened to shoot down an American spy plane. The two planes collided, and the Chinese pilot was lost at sea. The

American aircraft was forced to land on the Chinese Hainan Island. Relations between China and the United States became tense. As he had done in business, George W. Bush delegated responsibility. He tried to have the American ambassador to China handle the situation. Next, he got Secretary of State Powell involved. The Americans apologized for the loss of life of the pilot, but never conceded that the United States had done anything wrong. The crew and airplane were eventually released.

President Bush next tackled domestic issues. To show his bipartisanship, the President joined forces with Democratic Senator Ted Kennedy to pass a bill on education. In scientific research, Bush agreed to limited funding for stem cell research. However, when President Bush suggested drilling for oil in Alaska's wildlife area, there was strong opposition from Democrats and environmentalists. After negotiations with Congress, the president signed a tax cut bill of $1.6 trillion on June 7, 2001.

To meet heads of state around the world, Bush made trips through Europe and Asia in late spring of 2001. In Russia, President Putin and President Bush agreed to discuss the future of reducing the number of nuclear missiles. The President and Mrs. Bush met the Pope in Rome in July, and the president attended an economic summit of all the G-8 countries (the world's wealthiest industrial nations) in Genoa, Italy. There were violent demonstrations in the streets of Genoa against the meeting, against Bush, and against America.

Although Prime Minister Ariel Sharon of Israel met the president soon after his first month in office, relations between Israel and the Palestinians in the Middle East were at a breaking point. Suicide bombings by Palestinians and attacks by Israelis in response to the bombings worsened.

But the largest challenge for this president came only eight months into his administration. It would change him. It would change America. It would change the world.

TERRORIST ATTACKS

On Tuesday, September 11, 2001, the sky was a cloudless blue. The air was crisp and the sun was shining brightly in the aftermath of a hot summer. The Twin Towers of the World Trade Center in New York City stood tall and proud against the morning skyline. It was the beginning of a perfect September day.

In Boston, Logan Airport was filled with vacationers returning home, businessmen heading to California or elsewhere, and people traveling for various reasons. Around 8:00 A.M. American Airlines Flight 11 left Boston for California with 103 people aboard. Within minutes, it was hijacked by Arab terrorists, who turned the airplane south towards New York. At 8:45 A.M. this flight crashed into the north tower of the World Trade Center. United Airlines Flight 175 and its fifty-six passengers left Boston right behind Flight 11 and crashed into the south tower only minutes after 9:00 A.M. A fireball of flames and smoke from both towers billowed into the unblemished sky.

The steel and concrete structures spewed splintered glass and shards of concrete like a rain shower. Within an hour, the towers would collapse and disappear into a mangled pile of steel on the ground.

People on the streets were covered in ash and concrete dust. Police vehicles and fire trucks rushed to the scene. Firefighters and police officers ran into the buildings to save as many as they could. Almost three thousand people lost their lives in the towers, including three hundred firefighters and police officers. The nation was shocked as it had been over Pearl Harbor sixty years before.

Unfortunately, the horror wasn't over. United Airlines Flight 93 left Newark Airport at 8:01 A.M. It too was hijacked and directed toward Camp David or the Capitol or the White House. Some of the passengers

A person views the wreckage of the World Trade Center in New York City after the terrorist attacks.

on board decided to storm the cockpit and disable the Arab terrorists. At 10:00 A.M., the flight crashed into the ground just outside Pittsburgh, Pennsylvania. A fourth flight left Dulles International Airport in Washington, D.C. This was American Airlines Flight 77, headed for California. It departed at 8:10 A.M. At 9:43 A.M., after being hijacked, it crashed into a section of the Pentagon in Arlington, Virginia. Hundreds more people died in these fiery crashes.

President Bush was visiting an elementary school in Sarasota, Florida, that morning when his chief of staff, Andrew Card, interrupted. As he whispered the news to the president, Bush's face hardened. He excused himself and was whisked away in Air Force One to a safe location in the Midwest. Laura Bush was waiting to testify in the Senate about education. She and Vice President Richard Cheney were also taken to secure locations. The White House and capitol were evacuated. All air flights were grounded. The stock market closed and America virtually came to a standstill.

The terrorists were members of an extremist group called Al Qaeda headed by Osama bin Laden, a Saudi Arabian multi-millionaire, living in Afghanistan. The plan for these attacks had been in place for more than five years. The pilots had trained in Florida and Minnesota. The terrorists aimed to cripple the financial structure of the United States by destroying the World Trade Center; to cripple the U.S. military by striking the Pentagon, and probably to cripple the U.S. government by hitting the Capitol or the White House if the plan had been fully executed.

On Tuesday evening, President Bush spoke to the nation. He was strong, decisive, and focused. He declared the attacks as an act of war and promised to bring the terrorists to justice. At times Bush was presidential, but at other times, he was like a Texas sheriff seeking the outlaws "dead or alive." In the privacy of their White House quarters, Laura Bush advised her husband to "tone down" that last statement.

After the attacks on the World Trade Center in New York and on the Pentagon in Arlington, Virginia, President Bush delivers an address to the nation from the Oval Office on the night of September 11, 2001.

President George Bush offers encouragement to the workers at Ground Zero, the former site of the World Trade Center, in New York City on September 14, 2001.

On Friday morning, the president presided over a prayer service at the National Cathedral in Washington, D.C. George's parents and Laura sat beside him. Former president Bill Clinton and his wife along with Al Gore and his wife sat behind the Bushes. Churches everywhere held services and prayer vigils for our country.

On Friday afternoon, the president flew to New York City to see the devastation at the World Trade Center site known as Ground Zero. Someone handed him a megaphone. As he put an arm around a fireman's shoulders, George W. Bush delivered words of encouragement to the firefighters, police officers, and to all Americans. The cheerleader from Phillips Academy found himself cheerleading the people of his nation. Bitter rivalry in Congress was put aside. Democrats and Republicans embraced each other in national unity.

When later asked how September 11 had changed her son-in-law, Jenna Welch said sadly, "He doesn't smile as much anymore."

THE AFTERMATH OF TERROR

The recovery was slow and painful for the United States. George Bush took charge as a leader and gave many upbeat speeches. Tony Blair, Great Britain's prime minister, came to the president's aid immediately and declared his support. A coalition of countries was formed to free Afghanistan from the ruthless Taliban leadership and the Al Qaeda terrorist organization. The financial assets of the terrorists were immediately frozen.

Like his father before him, George W. Bush had a major war to face early in his administration. His father had enjoyed tremendous popularity during the Persian Gulf War. The son experienced similar popularity during the war in Afghanistan. However, the plunging economy after the Persian Gulf War had killed any chance of a second term for the elder Bush. To avoid the pitfalls that his father faced, George W. offered an economic stimulus package to ward off an economic failure of his own. It was passed in December of 2001. He offered a second stimulus in January of 2003 as the possibility of another war was developing.

In April of 2002, President Bush began an intensive campaign against Saddam Hussein of Iraq. He claimed that the Iraqi leader was hiding weapons of mass destruction that could harm the world. At first, public and world opinion opposed Bush's threat to directly attack Iraq. By late August and into the fall of 2002, President Bush tried to form a coalition with Europe and Great Britain. European countries were reluctant. He challenged the United Nations to assume responsibility it had neglected since the Persian Gulf War. After much resistance, Saddam Hussein agreed to open his country to inspectors in December. Still, the American public and many nations were not totally supportive of a war against Iraq.

During the same period, North Korea announced it would proceed to develop its nuclear weaponry in 2003 and resigned from the Nuclear Non-Proliferation Treaty. President Bush faced yet another serious challenge.

There were more challenges for the United States in March of 2003. Secretary of State Collin Powell appeared several times before the United Nations. He presented classified evidence of Iraq's possession of suspicious weapons of mass destruction. Despite his strong case, the countries of France, Germany, and Russia were opposed to an invasion of Iraq until the weapons inspectors had a longer time for examination. Only Great Britain's Prime Minister Tony Blair was a constant ally. At a national press conference in early March, President Bush expressed his intent to protect the United States from a biological, chemical, or nuclear attack by Iraq or by terrorists using Iraqi weapons. Without an international coalition or without U.N. support, Bush considered the possibility of American forces invading Iraq alone to remove the weapons. Over many months, the United States had assembled almost 300,000 troops in Kuwait and the surrounding area. Despite the ongoing worldwide criticism, the Bush administration achieved one major victory in March. The man thought to be Osama bin Laden's chief strategist for the September 11 attacks was captured in Pakistan. Khalid Shaikh Mohammed provided valuable information about the ongoing war of terrorism. Also, Bush called for a Palestinian state.

Later in the month, President Bush signaled the start of a war against Iraq to remove the mass destructive weapons and to change the ruthless regime, headed by Saddam Hussein, on March 19, 2003. Great Britain, under the leadership of Tony Blair, was the major ally in the military attack called Operation Iraqi Freedom. After several weeks of battle, President Bush announced an end to major combat in the war against Iraq on May 1, 2003. At the end of the war, the United States pledged to rebuild the country with the possible help of the United Nations and to establish a more just form of government.

If George W. Bush can restore the economy, control terrorism, and deal successfully with North Korea in 2003 and 2004, he could be reelected to a second term. If not, his place in history is still assured. His leadership during the worst acts of violence ever imposed on this country may make him a more acclaimed president than his father.

To a reporter from *Parade* magazine in April of 2001, George W. Bush was asked how he would like to be judged by history. The President replied, "All of us have God-given talents. And I think ultimately we'll be judged on whether we used those talents in a positive way or a destructive way. I hope it is written about me that I lived life to the fullest, that I realized my talents came from the good Lord and that I used them to make my community a better place."

The toddler from Texas, who became a wild teenager, a mediocre college student, an oil man, an owner of a baseball team, and governor of Texas, stepped out of his father's political shadow on September 11, 2001, to become a memorable forty-third president of the United States.

Timeline

1969 U.S. astronaut Neil Armstrong becomes the first person to walk on the moon.

1972 Five men are arrested for breaking into the Democratic National Committee's offices in the Watergate complex.

1973 George enters Harvard Business School.

1974 President Richard M. Nixon resigns as president of the United States.

1975 George graduates with an MBA from Harvard University and goes back to Midland, Texas, to find work in the oil business.

1977 He forms his own company, Arbusto Exploration.

George meets and marries Laura Welch, a teacher and librarian from Midland.

1978 George loses his race for U.S. House of Representatives.

1981 President Ronald Reagan is shot by John Hinckley Jr. on March 30, but later recovers.

George's twin daughters, Jenna and Barbara, are born.

1987–1988 George works on his father's campaign for president.

1988 George H. W. Bush is elected president of the United States.

1989 George buys a 1.8 percent share in the Texas Rangers baseball team for $600,000 and lives in Dallas as the managing general partner for five years.

1990 Iraqi forces invade Kuwait on August 2.

1991 The Persian Gulf War begins in January with the United States leading the effort to remove the Iraqis from Kuwait. A few months later, the Iraqis agree to a U.N. ceasefire, ending the conflict.

1994 George is elected governor of Texas with 53.5 percent of the vote.

1998 The baseball team is sold for $250 million and George receives over $15 million. He wins a second term as governor with a 68.6 percent landslide vote.

1999 George announces his intention to run for president of the United States against Vice President Al Gore.

2000 It takes thirty-six days from the circuit court to the Florida Supreme Court to the United States Supreme Court to determine George W. Bush as the winner of the 2000 presidential election.

2001 George is sworn in as the forty-third president of the United States.

Terrorists hijack airplanes and attack the World Trade Center in New York and the Pentagon in Washington, D.C. on September 11.

2002 Russia and the United States agree to reduce their nuclear arms arsenal. The FBI undergoes reorganization in intelligence gathering.

2002 George begins a campaign against Saddam Hussein of Iraq over weapons of mass destruction.

2003 North Korea withdraws from the Nuclear Non-Proliferation Treaty in January.

The United States, along with a small coalition of allies, started Operation Iraqi Freedom on March 19, a war against Iraq.

To Find Out More

BOOKS

Cohen, Daniel. *George W. Bush: The Family Business.* Brookfield, CT: Milbrook Press, 2001.

Marquez, Hero. *George W. Bush.* Minneapolis: Lerner Publishing Group, 2001.

Stone, Tania. *Laura Welch Bush: The First Lady.* Brookfield, CT: Milbrook Press, 2001.

ORGANIZATIONS AND ONLINE SITES

Biography of George W. Bush
http://www.whitehouse.gov/kids/president

More detailed information about the president is provided on this site.

George H. W. Bush Presidential Library
http://bushlibrary.tamu.edu

This gives extensive information on the forty-first president's library at College Station, Texas.

Internet Public Library
http://www.ipl.org/ref/POTUS/gwbush.html

This site gives a short biography of President George W. Bush and names his cabinet members. His key speeches are here, too.

Life in the White House
http://www.whitehouse.gov/kids/

This site is designed for children and has games and information about the president and first lady and videos of some of the rooms in the White House.

Photos of George W. Bush
http://bushlibrary.tamu.edu/photos/GWBush/index.html

This is a photo gallery of pictures of George W. Bush from childhood to adulthood.

Texas State History Museum
http://www.the storyoftexas.com/

Lots of good information on the history of the state of Texas is available on this site.

A Note on Sources

Before embarking on a research tour for my biography of George W. Bush, I read everything available on my subject. Knowing more about the person than about myself, I could begin the on-ground research with more confidence and knowledge. For every biography I write, I like to go to the country or the areas where my subject grew up. I want to see the homes and schools to be able to describe them for my readers. When the people I write about live in the United States, I travel in my small camper, accompanied by my two dogs. For the Bush book, I drove more than 5,500 miles. I stopped at Yale University and went to seven towns and cities in Texas to talk with relatives, friends, and teachers of George W. Bush. To actually see the landscape of Texas and to describe it, gave flesh and bones to my writing. Then, I drove to Phillips Academy in Andover, Massachusetts, to spend time in the archives before driving to Kennebunkport, Maine, where George W. spent summers. There are many adventures connected to every book I write. I keep two notebooks: one for professional notes and one for the personal experiences. In October of 2002, I met George W. Bush in Boston when he was campaigning for Mitt Romney, who was running for governor. I had a brief conversation with President Bush before he left. I found him to be personable, direct, and very proud of his family.

In terms of good resources for information on Bush, I would recommend *Barbara Bush: A Memoir. All the Best, George Bush: My Life and Other Writings, A Charge to Keep,* and *First Son: George W. Bush and the Bush Family Dynasty.* Newspapers and magazines, such as *The Boston Globe, The Christian Science Monitor,* and *Time* magazine, were also very helpful and supplied up-to-date information.

—*Libby Hughes*

Index

About the Author

Libby Hughes is an author, playwright, and drama critic. She received her bachelor's degree from the University of Alabama in Theater and English. Her master of fine arts degree was earned on full scholarship at Boston University. She freelanced for major newspapers in Africa and Asia for twelve years. Her biographies for young adults include books on Margaret Thatcher, Nelson Mandela, Colin Powell, Tiger Woods, Yitzhak Rabin, General H. Norman Schwarzkopf, Christopher Reeve, and Benazir Bhutto. Some of her plays and musicals have won prizes and been produced off-off-Broadway. She is listed in "Who's Who of American Women" and "Who's Who in the World." Hughes lives in Cambridge, Massachusetts, and on Cape Cod, writing books, plays, and musicals.